LIVING ALONE, LIVING TOGETHER

Two Essays on the Use of Housing

LIVING ALONE, LIVING TOGETHER

Two Essays on the Use of Housing

BY

PETER KING

Department of Politics and Public Policy,
De Montfort University, Leicester, UK

United Kingdom — North America — Japan
India — Malaysia — China

Emerald Publishing Limited
Howard House, Wagon Lane, Bingley BD16 1WA, UK

First edition 2017

Reprints and permissions service
Contact: permissions@emeraldinsight.com

British Library Cataloguing in Publication Data
A catalogue record for this book is available from the British
Library

ISBN: 978-1-78743-068-6 (Print)
ISBN: 978-1-78743-067-9 (Online)
ISBN: 978-1-78743-140-9 (Epub)

Printed and bound by CPI Group (UK) Ltd, Croydon, CR0 4YY

ISOQAR certified
Management System,
awarded to Emerald
for adherence to
Environmental
standard
ISO 14001:2004.

Certificate Number 1985
ISO 14001

INVESTOR IN PEOPLE

CONTENTS

ACKNOWLEDGEMENTS

This book, more than any other I have written, has depended on the kindness, steadfastness and love of other people. In revealing something of myself I have felt the need to seek the support of others for validation of this work. This book is about relationships and the (temporary) desire or need to withdraw from them. I therefore must acknowledge the massive debt I owe to my wife, B, and my two daughters, Helen and Rachel. They all feature in this work and have had the good grace to support me in writing it. B is a woman of tremendous strength and patience who deserves more than to live with a curmudgeon such as myself. My daughters have grown up surprising well despite their father. I thank them for continuing to endure, as well as to mock when they think I deserve it.

I am also very grateful to Jen McCall and her colleagues at Emerald Publishing for taking on such an eccentric work as this. Thanks also must go to the two anonymous reviewers who commented on an earlier draft of the book. As a result I think it is much improved and some of the grievous errors have been avoided.

Finally, I owe a tremendous amount to Roderick Evan, for opening up a pathway towards making sense of the dark and rather forbidding places I have at times been caught in. Because of him I have found a means of identifying and articulating what, for me, had been frustratingly elusive.

INTRODUCTION

A dwelling is a tool,[1] and policy is merely the subsidiary process that helps provide those tools. Housing is something that we use. We can focus on policies and on quantities; we can argue over white papers, spending targets and population projections, but what matters is how housing is used by those currently occupying it.[2] It is perhaps only natural that the predominant focus is on the material aspects of policies, quantities and standards: these are easy to see and to measure. We can contain these and so readily explain them. Reducing housing to quantities allows us to compartmentalise problems and posit easy solutions.[3] But, in doing so, we actually forget what housing is for. We can look at numbers built and their cost and feel that we have achieved something if there is some movement in these figures. Yet what matters just as much is how these dwellings are used. By this I don't mean that they are simply occupied — that square pegs are put into square holes — but in what ways do individual households take a dwelling and mould it to their purposes. In other words, how does a dwelling allow us to live? This, after all, is why we need a dwelling and why we attach any meaning to it.

As soon as we accept the importance of use, we also have to acknowledge that much of that use is both singular and private. It is not open to public scrutiny and would become impossible were it so observed. It literally does go on behind closed doors. Accordingly, it cannot be readily measured and quantified, and so we find it hard to generalise. All we have to go on are our own experiences and what others tell us of theirs. Yet, just because something is hard to see and even harder to measure does not mean it has no significance. Indeed, the significance of our dwelling to us is precisely because our use of it cannot be seen. We have, then, to find ways of looking inside that is not obtrusive, but which can still help us to capture the meaningfulness of our use of dwelling. Much of my work has been an attempt to find such a means,[4] and what I present here is my latest attempt.

This book consists primarily of two long chapters that present apparently contrasting views on the use of our dwelling. I say apparently because, while they appear to be opposites — on living alone and living together — they are actually complementary. To my mind they sit beside each other quite well. Like the poles of a magnet, which supposedly repel each other, they are actually connected and part of the same entity. Both chapters are concerned with how we are able to use private space. They are both based on a similar introspective method. Taken together they provide a more complete picture of how we can use our dwelling.

We live privately and have space that we say is ours. But much of this space is actually shared with a small number of others who we live with either through choice or accident of birth. We can relate to this space in an intensely subjective manner, and we know that others do too, and this is simply because we have direct corroboration — we can see how they behave. Much of the meaning that we derive from that space comes from who we share it with, but also because that sharing remains within private bounds.

But there is one place that we cannot share in any direct manner, namely the space inside our head. We can certainly describe our feelings to others and let them know what is going on in our headspace. Others may accept what we say as authentic and real. But ultimately that is because of what they know of us from the outside. They can have no knowledge of the actual inner space and instead have to rely on our facility with language and our ability to describe what we experience and feel. It is then incumbent on them to process what we say using their own headspace, allowing for how it is then sorted and filtered. We must accept the mediated nature of our description but we can seek to minimise it. We can try to reduce the level of mediation to the barest minimum and describe what is inside our own head and so leave the smallest amount for external interpretation. The listener or reader must still take much on trust, but they can test it against their own inner space with the minimum of iterations. This then is not a scientific approach and it has no pretensions to be so. All we can offer are a series of descriptions of particular head states.

The first of the major chapters in this book, 'On Living Alone', seeks to do this. It tries to describe what goes in in my head. There is certainly a cathartic element to this project, in that I have sought to understand my own head as a place that has often let me down. I have suffered from anxiety and depression for many years, and it has been a real problem for my wife and family as well as for myself. And this shows the connection right here: I cannot share my head with others, but I do share the place where I live. It is in this place that the contents of my head have much of their impact, and it is a shared place.

What I have found, however, when I talk to those closest to me about my depression (something incidentally I have been very loath to do until recently) is that I am perhaps the least aware of how I am and what I do (and perhaps this is because of my reluctance to discuss it). As I explain in the piece, when I am depressed I cannot think, and when I can think — which is when I am not depressed — the last thing I want to do is dwell on the bad times. So this work is a conscious effort to think through what it means to have a head that is sometimes out of control. This has been a very hard piece to write. Some of the material is more than 12 years old and I have been reluctant to deal with it. Other things I have written down about my depression I have not included here, it being simply too painful and close to the bone. It would involve exposing too much and I am not yet ready to share it with anyone. There are some things that I am not even prepared to write down. So this remains a partial picture, with a deal of dissembling and hedging of the painful parts. I have tried to describe my depression as clearly and accurately as I can. But it remains partial, with some elements picked out and others remaining hidden. What is not described here is how my head feels most of the time, including the period when I was able to write this piece. These are the mentally calm and quiet times when I am relatively happy and productive.

Over the years I have read a reasonable amount of the literature on anxiety and depression, particularly in philosophy and social thought. Some of this reading will be evident here, but often only to be criticised. In general, I have not found this literature terribly useful. It has certainly been of little help in terms of my own mental health. It did not seem to be about me, and as I wasn't interested in this subject from a purely intellectual perspective, then it seemed inadequate. More recently I have found the works of Emanuel Swedenborg to be of a considerable comfort personally, as well as offering a model of our mental life that is more intellectually satisfying.[5] His ideas are often implicit in what follows but I do mention him where it becomes overt and necessary.

As a work of introspection my approach has been to dwell on the fragments that I have found within my head and to make some order from them. I have thought long and hard about how to structure this chapter, and much of my efforts have gone into reordering the material in a number of different ways. I am conscious that there are times where I appear to contradict myself and that I speak in different voices and with a distinctly different tone. In the end I thought that the best way of presenting this material was in a manner that actually emphasised these contradictions and differences, and I have done this precisely because this is how my mind works. The style of this piece is actually demonstrative of the very issues I want to discuss.

The same applies to the second chapter 'On Living Together', in that the style is as important as the content. A single chapter, broken up into numbered but unnamed sections, seemed to me to be the most natural approach when I first had the idea of writing this piece and began planning it out and making notes. I had always envisaged it as a single piece where all the key issues are taken together. I wanted to make it clear that the parts of the chapter were equal in terms of their content and their connection to each other. I wished to create an immediate impression of this connectedness and I wanted it to be read all of a piece and not something that one dipped into. So what matters here is the overall impression of the piece and how it creates what I hope is a reasonably coherent whole. Of course, more could be said and much of this could have been said differently. But this is what I have wished to say and I am grateful for the opportunity of being able to present it here in this manner.

In terms of its contents, as the title of the chapter suggests, it considers now we live together. Ostensibly, this might seem to be the polar opposite of the first chapter, but as will become clear in reading the first chapter, the way I survive depression and anxiety is through living with others. This too adopts an introspective approach, but is also dependent on a number of my previous books, particularly *Private Dwelling*[6] and *In Dwelling*,[7] where I consider the issues of private dwelling and subjectivity in some detail. These books focus primarily on the issues of privacy and exclusion, laying a general groundwork, and so my aim in this chapter is to explore how these general facets of dwelling allow us to live with others. As in these earlier works, I have relied on my own experiences of living in private space. This is the only means I believe we can hope to understand what goes on, but, as I have stated already, I do appreciate that it does pose problems in terms of corroboration and generalisability. I have my own beliefs, attitudes and certainties. In terms of living together, my personal experience is largely reliant on what might be considered to be traditional heterosexual and monogamous family structures. I am well aware that my experiences are limited and that this might lead me into making certain conclusions that others might not share. But then, my experiences, and the conclusions I draw from them, could only be properly authentic if they were limited. This does not mean that I believe that any particular family type or sexual preference is superior to another. Rather, what I mean is that if my experiences are real and genuine they are necessarily limited to a certain range. My intention is not to state that there is only one form of relationship, but rather to suggest what it means to understand any relationship, in all its uniqueness and singularity, from the inside. It may be an approach with its limitations, and I may be accused of making generalisations that do not apply quite as readily as I believe they do, but as I hope will become clear in the reading of this chapter, there really is no alternative to this approach.

The final chapter, 'Alone and Together' is a brief yet, I hope, effective attempt at bringing these two sides of dwelling together, by showing that we can be alone precisely because we are with others, and that being together does not mean that we have to give up what it is that makes us what we are.

These chapters ask a lot of questions but provide rather fewer answers. This is because they are speculations, throwing out ideas and comments with the hope of eliciting some form of a response. Consistent with what I have written elsewhere,[8] this is an attempt to think properly and deeply about housing and to do so from the inside of housing rather than to engage it with pre-existing tools that might not fit properly the concepts I wish to explore.

However, what I do not wish to do here is to rehearse again the arguments from my former books. I have spent a considerable amount of time — and printers' ink — on describing and justifying a subjective approach to housing, and I do not wish to go over this again. Likewise, I have developed a methodological approach to housing in my book *In Dwelling*,[9] and instead of repeating this again here I want actually do the walking rather than the talking. An early reader of one of these chapters suggested that, while the subject matter was not out of line with much of housing discourse, I appeared to be completely rejecting the usual tools of analysis. In this way, the reader suggested, I was wiping the slate clean and starting again. Until I read this comment it had not occurred to me that my sources and approach were so unusual and that I was trying to do anything quite so fundamental. I saw the approach I have now taken as a natural development from my earlier work: I was actually doing what I said housing researchers ought to do in *In Dwelling*. This was precisely to create concepts from out of housing rather than relying on 'off the peg' theories and concepts from other disciplines and which were intended for other purposes than analysing housing phenomena. But also these chapters have been inspired by my reading over the last few years, which in some ways could not be further from the mainstream housing studies literature. I suppose this does suggest an attempt to look at the issues in a distinctly new way, but this was for no other reason than this approach now seemed to be the most interesting and fruitful one for me to pursue. The results are doubtless unorthodox, but I hope that they will be read with an open mind and given the space that allows them to speak on their own terms.

NOTES

1. Heidegger (1962).

2. King (2017).

3. King (1996).

4. See in particular King (1996, 2004, 2008, 2017).

5. See Swedenborg (1987, 1996, 2010).

6. King (2004).

7. King (2008).

8. King (2017).

9. King (2008).

ON LIVING ALONE

There is one place where we know we can retain our privacy, where no one else can enter, where we can keep our secrets. But it is a dark and mysterious place. It is a place where we can be ourselves, but it is also a place we struggle to understand. It is ours but we often cannot control it. It can confound us, confuse us and let us down. But no one else need know the slightest thing unless we let it slip. The place I am referring to is the inside of our head.

Of course, properly speaking, it is not a place at all. The inside of our head is full of organic matter. There is no real space that we can stretch out in or explore as we might a building or a neighbourhood. To call it a place is already to revert to metaphor. It is a 'place' of thoughts, feeling, emotions and dreams, not somewhere we can actually walk around in.

Despite this, I want to insist that it really is somewhere we can go to. In a very real sense we are in there. It is the most private place that we can go to, where we can be free from all others and where we can hide. If I don't tell anyone what is in my head it can never be known. So we are, or can be, truly alone with our thoughts.

But sometimes it feels like there are competing voices in my head, pushing and pulling in different ways. They contradict each other and leave me confused. They make demands and then deny responsibility; they pull me one way and then mock me for following them.

My head is the place where I plot, plan, think, reflect, and all in perfect privacy. It is a place where I can really be alone. But it is a place I cannot really control. Our head seems to have an infinite storage capacity, but an inconsistent and perverse retrieval system. It is full of tunnels, trapdoors, hidden rooms, inaccessible corridors, detours and misleading directions. Often there is only a dim light or even darkness. We soon find then that we cannot really trust it.

And why does a mood swing, something that we all have from time to time, turn itself into an illness? When does the apparently normal shift in our behaviour turn into depression? Is it merely a matter of turning up the volume? Why, to get to the point, are my private thoughts often overtaken by anxiety and depression?

My headspace gives me a lot of trouble. It may be inaccessible and uncontrollable to others, but it is also often like this for me too. Much of what goes on in there is a mystery to me. I do things I don't wish to, that I know I will later regret. It creates uncertainty and false certainties, false images of myself and of others. It tells lies to me. It leads me astray. It makes me depressed.

Perhaps we have actually less control over our head than the place we live in. We can move house, but we cannot move head. Our head is not so easy to traverse or navigate; it is much harder to tidy up or re-arrange; and we cannot move out to somewhere else: we can't downsize as we get older. We are stuck with the one place all our lives. We even inherit a lot of baggage from our parents, and so we don't even get to choose the décor and layout ourselves.

§

So no one but me is inside my head. Why then does it often feel that there is more than one person in there? There seems to be different parts or versions of me competing for space inside my head. These versions seem to be in conflict: there is the good versus the bad, the benign against the selfish, the outward looking battling the inwards, the contented and optimistic me against the alienated and anxious one. At different times one of these versions of me is dominant, and, of course, not always the good ones. We might see this as a battle between angels and devils, good or evil spirits, good or bad ideas, or as different personas. But they are all, properly speaking, *me*. At any precise moment I do not feel particularly different. It still seems to be me in there. What does differ is the outside world, or rather how it appears: whether it is benign or hostile; whether it is for me or against me; whether it understands me or seems to disregard everything I say or do. What differs is how the world seems to engage with me: does it take me as a member of the human race or as an alien with little in common with it? It often feels as if it is just me against the world. But I, so I tell myself, so I insist, have not changed.

I can only deal with this apparent hostility in one of two ways: by generating my own hostility — anger, rage, shouting back — or by hiding away from the world, by withdrawing, skulking and sulking, by effectively switching off and hibernating away and curling up into a little foetal ball under a blanket and sleeping. I either lash out or I close down. The latter is the most common, but sometimes it follows a short outburst of anger. The anger soon turns inwards, as a sense of simmering resentment against everyone and everything, and I withdraw. In this state everything appears to be monochrome, a uniform grey. I am at the bottom of a well with no clear way out and indeed without any real intention of trying to get out — it is a well I have dug myself, of my own making, even as I resent where, and how, I am. There is no means of escape and no point in trying. I accept where I am and wait for it to pass — I can do this because it is not my fault — muttering some resentful dirge to myself.

At these times I feel totally, completely, absolutely, resolutely alone, and this is even the case if others are with me in the same room. There is no longer any connection, any warmth, any light, anything radiating in or out of me at all. There is just this grey hole with me at the bottom.

How do I come out of this state? And why does it happen when it does? Do I have any choice over this? Perhaps life could simply not go on for long in this grey well. From time to time I need to come up to the surface to replenish myself. This though suggests that the grey well might be the default state, and I couldn't bear to think that.

What does often draws me out — what makes me act differently — is the pull of tenderness: my connection with my wife and children. My feelings towards them start to bear down on the greyness and then come to overpower and dominate it. But why does this happen? Why does life suddenly (or eventually) come to seem positive and benign again? Why cannot I feel this all of the time?

In truth, both the good and the bad sides of me remain present: it is just that one can come to dominate, and I can seemingly do little to control the situation. Sometimes the volume just gets turned up too far. Over the years though I have found no real trigger, no reason for it. I can seldom see the period of greyness coming and predict it. Likewise, I tend to have no inkling of it ending. I am either on one side or the other, completely one and nothing of the other (or so it seems: things are always only as they seem). There is no gradual or gentle slide from one to the other. Yet, at the same time, I do feel a continuity: it is the same *me* all the time. There is an internal continuity and a feeling that it is the world that now appears to react differently to me and for no reason that I can fathom.

There is something childish in this sense of the world not understanding me, of it actively colluding against me. I cannot get my own way and it is simply so unfair. Sometimes, always afterwards, I can see that this is intensely selfish, as purely wilful, just sulking because I cannot get my way. It then seems all too clear — until the next time.

§

Don't you ever feel afraid? Do you not sometimes feel so lost, abandoned and without anything left to hope for? Is there not sometimes just too much world, such that you are in danger of being overwhelmed? What then do you do? Where do you go? Where do they find you?

§

Why do we withdraw? Why do we close the door and shut the curtains? Is it just to keep warm? Or is it so that we can be properly alone, alone with ourselves and those we love, alone together, or just alone?

§

Enclosure provides us with the antidote to loneliness. The boundaries, just as they keep us apart, help us to forget, and because they enclose, they help us to feel safe within. What we want to forget is now outside, away from and beyond the boundaries. It — they — are not with us, *they are not us*. They are apart from us.

§

Being alone — away from them, the world, those who don't care — helps us to forget that we might be lonely. We can forget the crowds that are indifferent to us. We can be at the centre, the very heart of things, even as we have restricted it so as only to include ourselves. We are the one who now make things tick. Indeed, we are the world now, held and enclosed against whatever others might try to implicate us in.

§

There is always a bad side and a good side. It is our mutual indifference (stating it negatively) or our mutual respect for others (being positive) that allows us to control our immediate environment. We are left alone and have our aloneness respected by others, most of whom are doing precisely the same as we are. It is not that we wish to ignore others, or that we do not care. Rather it is that we are more concerned for some particular ones and wish to prioritise our care for them. This creates an unintended exclusivity that allows others to proceed without interference from us.

§

What are we alone for? Why are we without others? Perhaps it is because we choose to be. We reject the company of others and choose to live away from them, letting distance exclude us. It might be that we wish to be free of all responsibility and not be held back by others. We wish only to focus on ourselves. Perhaps we wish to achieve enlightenment and some link with the transcendent. Or it might be that we need to detox and to start looking after ourselves properly. Less dramatically, it might be that we are too busy with our career or other interests, which preclude contact with others and so we cannot form relationships. It might be that our obsessions prevent us from seeing others. Then again, we might be alone because we simply cannot find anyone despite looking very hard. No one, we think, is good enough for us. No one meets our expectations of what our lifelong partner should be like. So we choose to be alone rather than put with what we take as second best.

Or it might be that we have no choice. We would love to be with others but are constantly rejected or ignored by them. We might lack the social skills to link with others. We are incurably shy or feel that we are inadequate in some way. Or we may be being punished for our past actions, even to extent of being literally imprisoned and in solitary confinement. But being ignored by others need not be deliberate, but merely that everyone else chooses to be elsewhere and with other people rather than us. We might not be actively rejected but just a victim of indifference.

We might be alone due to bereavement, where we have lost those closest to us. Or we might be alone because of illness of incapacity: we cannot get out to see others and there is no one to come to see us. Both of these might only be temporary, in that grief and illness are things that we can recover from. So this period of isolation might be a transitional phase and, in time, we can connect again.

§

Can we be alone together? Can we be with someone or in a group, but still be alone, where we are not linking with anyone properly, having nothing in common with anyone, being semi-detached from the group, looking on from the periphery, commenting perhaps, assessing, evaluating the group from the edge rather than being a full part of it? We might hold ourselves back for some reason, be it reticence, arrogance, or some other reason. We just cannot commit to the group. We are in the company of others but not really with them. We are still apart and may appear to others to be reserved, haughty, or even hostile. We lack any conviction to participate and to be included. We could quite easily detach ourselves, which might not, because of our reserve, even be much noticed by the others.

In being with others we might be led more by habit and routine than by conviction. Or it might be that we are obliged formally to be a part of a group as part of our studies, our employment or our family commitments. We have to be there, because of the decisions we have made in the past: we want to pass our course, we need to build our career and have money to pay the mortgage, we feel we ought to have some affinity with relatives. But we still have little in common with these people we are with and would not necessarily choose to be in their company were we not so committed.

In might be that we were once closer to others, but we have drifted apart from them. It may be that as teenagers we seek more distance from our parents and siblings. Or it might be where a couple's interests diverge over time and once the children have left find they have less in common than they thought they had. But even as they drift apart they stay together — there is still something that holds them. This may be due to habit, inertia, or financial necessity. But, more positively, it may be that we still love and care for these people because of the shared history and memories. There remains an accumulated affection and common trust. At times we might notice the drift, but we maintain the relationship because it is where we are and who we are. We are comfortable still with them. There is still enough to keep us together and committed, even if this is for negative rather than positive reasons or simply the weight of years. We are still at home, amongst what is known, stable and comfortable. We cannot contemplate giving this up.

Indeed we often have no real alternative. Where else would we go? We may not be able to afford change even if we wished it. But even so, we may not feel trapped. We might be mildly disappointed, dissatisfied and disaffected, but not exactly unhappy. We do not consider ourselves to be alone. We can still rely on the others around us and we can offer support and comfort to them.

Yet, in a certain way, we are alone. We may be together physically, but not emotionally or spiritually: we do not really share our lives with others anymore. All we share are the routines and the space they take place through and in.

Of course, it is very rare to be completely together — to be *always* together — with another. We do not always act together as one. We might even say that complete togetherness is not always healthy. We might benefit from some time alone and some space to simply be ourselves. All relationships have their differences in terms of interests, beliefs, opinions and priorities. We may not feel precisely the same about each other: one might feel more connected and committed than the other. In most cases this will not matter. We retain our individuality and do not become overtaken by another or become subsumed into something else. Indeed, we might suggest that being in a relationship with a particular other actually makes some statement about us as a differentiated individual.

§

Anxiety is a state of uneasiness where we are concerned over an imminent danger or difficulty, over something that troubles us. To say we are anxious means we are worried that things might change, that something will or is about to happen or it might be a worry that things will not change and not get any better, that there is no way out of our predicament. But anxiety is often general or non-specific. It frequently takes the form of a generalised sense of unease rather than a specific fear or worry. Anxiety need not be directed at anything specific, although, at any one time, we may think that it is quite specific. This suggests it is within us, and hence the usefulness of the image of a tight ball or knot inside us. We tend to be anxious and experience this serially rather than it being caused by something purely external and specific. We are prone to anxiety in general rather than it arising from a single and temporary cause. It might be best therefore to see it as a disposition or an illness and not a particular reaction to circumstance.

Anxiety then comes from within us instead of from some external cause. While a fear might be imposed on us, our anxieties are what we impose on ourselves by attaching it to some external entity. Anxiety is where we have a sense of dread, which may be attached at one time to something specific but then we find it has moved on to something else.

We can see anxiety as where we cannot contain a situation. The situation goes beyond us and we feel we are not in control of it. The object of anxiety looms out at us and we cannot suppress our feelings, which continue to grow. We have no proper sense of proportion or means of keeping issues within bounds or to place them in their proper context. The object of anxiety so pervades our consciousness that we cannot see beyond it. To achieve this object, or to survive it, to get past it, is all that matters to us. What we tend to forget, to lose sight of in our anxiety, is that this object — be it a journey, a meeting, lecture, or whatever — is usually only a stage in a process, a means to achieve something larger, part of a series of events and objects to negotiate towards a greater aim. Yet we cannot see this, our anxiety masks this from us, so we cannot see it as it is.

Of course once the journey or event is over and we have achieved it, we can then see it for what it is and that our anxiety was misplaced and unfounded. The journey was indeed straightforward and we can now appreciate that what matters more is what we can do on our arrival. Anxiety can be controlled, or put into proportion, only in hindsight. We cannot deal with it in advance. And so this tiny victory, of apparently beating anxiety by doing what we dreaded, does not necessarily stop us feeling anxious the next time we go on a journey or face a similar meeting. Hence it really is significant to see anxiety as coming from inside and not dependent on external circumstances. Anxiety is very adept at finding its own stimulation.

§

Do I spend too long on the inside, too long on introspection? Why am I hidden away in my own headspace and not in the outside world? Is it that I can actually find enough within my own headspace that I don't need to go out, that almost my entire world is there? Should I find comfort in this?

§

Waking up anxious again! What for? What have I to worry about? Why have I woken up now?

But then why does there have to a reason? Why do I have to be anxious about anything in particular? My anxiety, it seems to me, is often general and non-specific. It has no point of focus, no target. I do not think I am anxious about anything. It seems instead that anxiety picks the nearest thing and inflates it. Or perhaps I am anxious about everything — of just being here and still having to face the world.

But here I am, at 4.00 in the morning, in the dark and prickling with anxiety, tossing and turning, worrying about I know not what. Slowly it will fade, or nearly always it will, and come morning I feel OK if hardly refreshed, and able to face something of the day.

Does anxiety ever need a purpose? Does it have an end in mind, or can it be just there, that anxiety *just is*, as an end in itself. It is a separate thing, a person in itself, another 'me' that feeds off the rest.

Being anxious is enough in itself. It does not need to go any further and to attach itself to anything more concrete. From its point of view, the more general and nebulous it remains the better. It just sits there in my head, weighing me down as I lie there immobile yet all too alert.

I want this anxiety out of my head. I want to be free of it. I want calm, peace and quietness and not this constant fluttering in my head, like a moth clattering inside a lampshade.

Yet it has to be said that I lead a remarkably stress-free life — or rather I ought to. I work at home for half the week and I love my job, my family and where I live. I am able to spend most of my time talking, reading or writing about things that really interest me. I can set my own agenda to a large extent. I don't have that many meetings to attend. I travel to and from work on the train as I have done thousands of time over the last 25 years, and this gives me more time to read or to write. I really have very little to be anxious about.

But anxiety seems to work in its own way and can make use of whatever material is available. It creates its own scales of intensity out of what it can find. If travelling on a route I have done countless times is all it has, then it will find a means of using it; if there is marking still to be done or a meeting to attend then it will pick these as targets.

And yes, I do see anxiety as a thing, almost as a distinct entity or animate being of some sort that uses me for its purposes. This anxiety is *not* me, and it is very important for me to believe it is not me. It is like a virus attacking me. The virus affects me, *but it is not me.*

When I am anxious any movement, any commitment, can appear daunting and involve an epic journey that presents me with a huge challenge. I have to cross a huge and dangerous chasm to get where I need to be. There is no sense of proportion here, nothing rational or considered.

Anxiety strikes because I am alone, or feel alone, and it magnifies that feeling. It comes at night when my guard is down, when everyone else is asleep. My anxiety will not let me wake up anyone to seek help, and so I have to face it down or to ride it out and see where it takes me. Neither option is easy or comfortable.

When the anxiety is gone — and so far it always has gone — it feels like it will never again be there. It seems so very alien and distant from where I now am. I forget about it as quickly as I can, and so it is a real effort to write about it. I am trying to remember what it is like to be in a place where I never aim to go again. When I am there the last thing I wish to do is write about it. I have no energy, no patience and

I lack the vocabulary to describe it. Now as I write it feels like I am dealing with someone else's symptoms. It is a different person and all I can do is somehow approximate the feelings and sensations. I cannot be sure how accurate I am in my assessments and whether this is anything but a very partial insight. It seems to me that I am being a bit too general and lacking in specificity, that I am not getting it totally right. But what else can I do here (other than, of course, leaving it alone entirely)? How much closer can I get than actually being in the same head?

The difficulty for me is precisely because I see continuity rather than distinction or difference. It seems always to be the same me, and so how can I be different from how I now am? I am always 'as I now am'. This delusion means that, apart from this partial hindsight, I can never get outside of the anxious me and analyse it with any real certainty. The very lack of detachment that I need to maintain my sense of self means that I cannot separate out one part from another: I cannot distinguish one version of me from another. To me now, and it is always 'now', I am just being me as I am. I might regret this intellectually, but it is, or so it seems, a necessary requirement to preserve myself mentally.

So, to try and understand my anxiety, I have to rely on memory, and I know that this cannot always be trusted, and this is precisely because I try so hard to forget my anxiety when I can exist without it. I never wish to return to that state and I always feel that I never will again. As much as I know it is part of me, it feels now completely alien and very distant and it will never be here again. It is simply not possible I could be that type of person, who thinks those thoughts and feels that way. This attitude, as delusional as it might be, is necessary if I am to continue on: if I had to admit to the absolute certainty of a return to anxiety then I would become frozen and incapable of acting. When I am free of anxiety that is how I will always be and so why then wallow in what is past and what I cannot now affect. Why dwell on the past when I have an optimistic present to wallow in? My wife will often try to talk about it, and she needs to, as she is often the one who is bruised by the experience. But I have no desire or patience for this. It is the very last thing I wish to dwell on now I am out of it. I just want to get on with the positive parts of my life and leave the nasty bits behind. I want no autopsy, no raking over the issues. I want to move on and move away from the scene of my depression.

§

According to Martin Heidegger,[1] anxiety and fear are different things: fear is always of something, whilst anxiety is groundless, it has no purpose. Anxiety reveals to us that we are not at home in the world and that we are facing something that is not quite right, that is uncanny, or as it is in German, *unheimlich*, unhomelike. Anxiety, Heidegger tells us, relates to finitude, to our so called 'being-towards-death'. We realise that we cannot escape the concerns of the world, and that we can never be free of our own mortality.

Heidegger did not see anxiety as a subjective psychological state, but part of the structure of existence. Anxiety comes from living in the world. It is not an illness or a particular problem an individual might have to face because of particular circumstances. It is an ontological rather than psychological condition, and so Heidegger seems to externalise anxiety. But this seems to take no account of the nature of anxiety as we experience it as individuals. It does not explain why anxiety increases and decreases *in me*, or why it differs from person to person. Why are some more people anxious than others? Heidegger can offer us with no comfort, but then perhaps he never meant to.[2]

§

On either side of the millennium it became popular amongst social theorists and others to argue that we were living in a risk society or in the age of anxiety.[3] We were apparently becoming more anxious as we faced uncertainties over climate change, globalisation and terrorism. These writers used an apparent increase in the use of prescription drugs and the growth of social movements as indicators of a general increase in anxiety. So, for example, Renata Salecl, in her book *On Anxiety*, describes a general increase in anxiety that occurred after September 11. In order to build this kind of argument, however, anxiety has to be seen as generalised, and so effectively collectivised. Anxiety is related to some general cause, in this case the terrorist attacks on New York and Washington in 2001, through simplistic measurements such as the use of anti-depressants and other drugs in the immediate period after. There may indeed have been some link between these two phenomena, but there is a problem, and this is that anxiety is not a collective entity. Anxiety is something that is internal to an individual, and which is then attached onto external entities. It arises because of a particular disposition within specific people and is not simply created by external stimuli. Clearly, events can affect how people feel, and extreme events can have considerable consequences. Yet, anxiety is still something that is generated within, and so it exists independently of any external event. As an individual I may feel more or less anxious and this, we might suggest, could be added to the general stock of anxiety to show an overall increase. But it is still me and not society or humanity in general that is anxious. Society does not take Prozac, individual sufferers do.

In any case, what does it mean to say that anxiety is on the increase? Can it be dealt with in utilitarian terms, so that greater numbers means it is worse? If more people are taking anti-depressants does that necessarily mean that anxiety has increased? To take what is perhaps the most obvious problem with this simplistic association, it takes no account of the level of anxiety. Might it be that a large number of people with relatively low levels might present a lower level of total anxiety than a smaller number with a higher intensity? So we might have a society that has smaller numbers of cases of anxiety, yet the total sum of anxiety still is greater. For example, let us suspend our disbelief for a moment and suppose that we can measure anxiety by some numerical ordering such that 1 is low and 5 high. By averaging the level of anxiety across a population and counting the numbers we could then come up with some total level of anxiety. We can imagine two societies, one (society A) consisting of 1,000,000 with an average intensity of 2, and the other (society B) consisting of 500,000 people with an average anxiety of 5. According to one measure society A has twice the level of anxiety as society B. Yet if we also measure the intensity using our hypothetical units we see that there are two million units of anxiety in society A but 2.5 million in society B. So a smaller society might actually have higher levels of anxiety due to the specific nature of the problems they are facing (e.g. compare Syria with Britain).

This, of course, assumes that we can measure anxiety in a common form and that it is not prey to cultural factors or changing patterns of diagnosis and treatment. But how might we try to measure it? The most obvious is the one we have already mentioned, namely, the number of prescriptions for the relevant drugs. Yet there are so many variables that will affect this such as the cost of treatment, and the ability of all members of a society to gain access to them (which means that a more affluent society might show a higher incidence due to a greater ability to access drugs), the availability of doctors and their preparedness and ability to deal with anxiety compared to other priorities. So while anxiety would be a big problem in Aleppo, it might remain a low priority compared to treating shrapnel wounds. But we might, however, use other medical data to supplement that of the uptake the drugs, such as the levels of suicide, self-harm and general violence in a society. So we might assume that anxiety goes along with the shrapnel wounds.

The literature on risk and anxiety also points to other more indirect means such as the number of incidents that are said to cause anxiety such as natural disasters and acts of terrorism, or the growth in membership of protest groups opposing nuclear weapons, globalisation and environmental degradation. But, in the latter case, there may be plenty of other factors that have led to the growth of these groups such as the decline of mainstream political parties. It is also the case that in some societies, where anxiety levels might be quite high, there is not the freedom of association and civil liberties that allow for the formation of these groups.

But what we are still ignoring here is that anxiety impacts on individuals. It is not suffered collectively but within the heads of individual people. Even in Aleppo there will be some people who show no signs of anxiety, while even in the most cossetted of societies there will be some who suffer chronically. Of course, we should be concerned if there is an apparent increase in anxiety, just as we should were there an increase in broken limbs. This can have an impact on scarce health care resources and might indicate some changing pattern of behaviour. But, just as we would treat each broken limb on its own merits regardless of this changing pattern, the same applies with anxiety. Anxiety, despite what we might think, is not contagious.

But it might be that what writers like Salecl are referring to a rather different thing from what I have described as anxiety? As we have suggested, anxiety comes from inside us and attaches itself to a specific issue. This external showing is therefore just a symptom, its outward manifestation, and not the cause of anxiety. Anxiety, then, is not a social malaise but an illness. What Salecl and others are referring to is essentially a heightened sense of political risk, which may then, but not necessarily will, be a target for an internal state of anxiety.

§

I do share my anxiety, but only its affects. I share, or rather distribute, the anger, sullenness, unreasonableness and the argumentativeness. But for others it lacks the proper context. There is none of the pain that sparks the anger and distress. They cannot see what causes me to behave in this manner. For them it is all affects and no cause. It is therefore very hard for anyone, who has not suffered depression themselves, to appreciate what it might be like, and often it is hard to react with any sympathy. One has to know the person very well, to be aware of their potential for good actions as well as bad ones, in order to forgive them and still be there.

§

Anxiety, for me and for many, is never, so to speak, quite bad enough. It is bad enough to affect my life and of those around me. But it never lasts long enough, or is of such an intensity, to be so unbearable that I wish to give up. There is always room to endure it a bit more. This might be a relief — it will not kill me — but it does mean that I will have to live with it. Anxiety, it seems, knows well enough how to keep its host alive.

§

Our mind is accessible only to us, even if we cannot control it as we would like. No one has access to our headspace but us. We have to mediate between it and others. We have to tell others what is in there, what it is like and we can decide to give as much or as little information as we please. We decide and no one else has access. It is, then, perhaps the only really private space we can have. We share only what we want and do so only on our terms. We can think what we like regardless of what we are told and taught. No one can know what we have thought, unless we choose to tell them, and even here we might lie, dissemble or merely give a partial explanation. We are under no obligation to divulge all we have been thinking. And even if we were so obliged, there can be no independent corroboration. I have to accept what another tells me they are thinking. I may feel it to be implausible; I may think they are lying, but I do not really know and can have no means of finding out until events unfold.

So my head is *my* space. It is not shared and it is not readily accessible to anyone else. It can stay closed. And this applies to any form of mind control or torture: It still depends on us telling others what is in there and there is no means to check that we are really being honest or telling the whole story.

We are all separate and distinct beings, even those who share considerable parts of their lives with others and whom we know very well. They still have secrets and we can never know what it is that is really being thought behind the mask they present to us. We may think that we know the minds of others; that we know what they are thinking and what their motives are and that we can read them. At times we may even be right. But we are always guessing, making certain assumptions about the behaviour and actions of others. We cannot be sure and this applies even if they say we are right. We have to believe in their honesty and that they aren't lying or concealing something, or simply haven't forgotten some basic element. They might be deluded or ill. There are many occasions where people of good will are mistaken or deluded for reasons that are not malicious or even conscious. People may get facts wrong even when they are certain that they are correct. We can convince ourselves of many things when we are alone with our thoughts.

And this is what we always are: alone with our thoughts. When we try to describe our thoughts it is the same as describing a person to someone else who has not met them, and then expecting the listener to recognise them when they see them. No matter how accurate we may be this is not the same as the actuality of pointing to that person and saying 'Look, that is her there'. Our description is not the same as spending time in the company of that person and really getting to know them, their mannerisms, sense of humour, way of speaking, their likes and dislikes. But in the case of thoughts we can only ever describe them. There is not the expedient of a photograph or a real life meeting. There is no independent access to our thoughts beyond our own description of them. We can never, so to speak, be face-to-face with the thoughts of another or hear them for ourselves.

§

Much of the time I survive anxiety by self-exclusion, by opting out and not taking part. This means that there are no expectations on me. One of the few times I can find comfort while I am anxious is when I have nothing planned, and so have total freedom to do what I want and avoid anything that might be a source of stress. Of course, this is a very rare occurrence: most of the time, like anyone else, I have commitments I cannot avoid. But there is often no correlation between the level of anxiety I feel towards a commitment I have and whether I actually find it stressful or enjoyable at the time. The problem is entirely in having to do anything at all. Most of these commitments, in any case, are relatively minor, routine and involve things I have already done countless times, such as visiting people or going to meetings, but they can loom so large that at the time they seem to be quite unmanageable. Yet, others things such as talking to a large crowd of relative strangers about my work does not worry me unduly. I will get nervous, but it remains in bounds and is not a source of anxiety.

§

I have to admit that I often prefer to be alone. Most of the pursuits I have are solitary ones that do not involve communication with others, such as reading, watching sport, films, listening to music and writing. My work is also often solitary. I do rely on others, but not in a direct and collaborative way. I do not feel being on my own is much of an issue for me. I enjoy the company of my wife and children and would lay down by life for them without thinking. Yet often they will be doing something together while I am doing something on my own. This was never conscious. I have not been actively excluded and nor have I taken myself off deliberately. Likewise, I have no difficulty in talking with others: it is what I do for a living. But I am a solitary person and often like to be on my own. I can find comfort in a book or a film and I do not feel I am being left out of anything. This is doubtless linked in some way to my depression, but I am not sure which came first. However, there has been a slow drift into solitude over the years.

§

Anxiety magnifies the self. It forces us inwards and our own concerns, problems and general state grow to subsume all else. It is a form of narcissism: we only have regard for ourselves. It can make us appear selfish and wilful as we only focus on ourselves and exclude all others. We appear to contain all of the world that we need: We are self-contained and able to ignore anything else.

Anxiety, then, appears to encourage selfishness, to encourage dwelling on ourselves. Only our problems matter, everyone else's are not real; no one can really understand us and what we are going through, and nor are they really trying.

We might come to believe that the outside world is full of fools, idiots and half-wits out to torment us. In this way anxiety leads us to disregard the merits and interests of others. In so far as we even recognise they exist, we feel that they are there merely for us, and even here they tend to fail us. They might come to pose a threat to us through their lack of understanding and because they seem to be working against our interests, and so we need to defend ourselves. We need to take shelter, to arm ourselves against the world. We need to hunker down and wait out this winter of hostility.

Accordingly, we do not seek the help of others. It does not occur to us to turn to them. We cannot trust them. Instead we face inwards and ignore others, even as they may be trying to help us. We seek what solace we can from within. Of course, if we consistently refuse help then it may well stop being offered. But this merely serves to prove out initial point that everyone is against us.

§

There are times when I simply cannot get out of my head. This, or so it seems to me, is not because of what is inside my head, and whether it is interesting, good for me or whatever, but because of what I perceive as going on outside it. The world is unreliable, inconsistent, an unpleasant and nasty place. But my head is where I can always safely be, where I always am and where I am always accepted. My head can always accommodate me.

But my head might not be the best place for me to be. It might not be the most reliable of environments to hang around in. For example, it might not be the best place to get accurate, unbiased and reliable information. It might not always, or even often, have the right answers. It might trick me, or it might try to be honest but is in fact deluded. So I can't just rely on it and expect things to go just as I would hope.

This is the problem of cutting oneself off from others: We might not be prey to certain influences that cause us trouble, but instead we have come to rely on a single source, and cannot really be sure that it can be trusted. Does our head really know what is going on? Where does it get its information from? Not going out much might make us feel safe but it also does not help us in understanding the world around us.

But it is even more complex than this. If we do seek information from outside of our head, where do we put it once we have it? Where do we store it and what do we use to make sense of what we have found out in the world?

The only filter we have is within our heads. This may serve to protect us from potential contaminants, but it also helps us to maintain our delusions. It sifts out what is unpalatable and uncomfortable and lets us focus on what we feel supports us and justifies our prejudices. The filter is always there, but sometimes it seems to let more or less material in. Sometimes more seems to get through, while at other times there seems to be a complete block. It might also be the case that what does get through is altered by the process, by the method of filtration, such that it cannot be relied upon. It might have been changed to fit what we now find acceptable, and which supports an existing mental picture. We only let through what doesn't jar with our existing views, or which doesn't challenge our prejudices. We have built up a particular picture of the world and our filter now serves to maintain that and deal with any potential challenges. Our mental filter is now concerned with confirmation rather than information.

But even if this information has been so repackaged it still, because of the process of filtration, appears understandable to us. We have so re-arranged it that it makes perfect sense. But this is only because of what it confirms. Those elements that might disabuse our picture of the world are not allowed through.

This mental filter is akin to that used on a camera lens, but one that has different setting or levels of intensity. It only lets certain things through but, like a lens filter, it can also change or intensify certain colours to create a particular effect. In black and white photography a red filter can be used to darken the sky creating the effect of a heavy and dramatic atmosphere. A polarising filter will deepen the colour blue and can also be used to deal with glare. It can allow us to see things more clearly. A polarising filter can be adjusted to heighten or lessen particular effects. So we can keep out parts of the light spectrum or intensify the effects of light in order to alter how we see — and show — the world.

We might see depression as where a grey filter comes across our vision and so we see everything as grey-tinted. Everything is dulled and what is already dark is darkened further. There is less of a contrast between light and shade or rather the grey turns light into shade.

What causes the grey filter to come across and alter how we see things? It does not appear to be there always, or at least it does not have the same intensity such that it can pass without notice. But perhaps it is always there, and it is merely the case that sometimes the strength is increased so that it obviously and clearly affects what we can see.

However, regardless of this, the onset of depression for me is not a slow process. There is no cycle or rhythm to it, and accordingly I can never see it coming. The filter just comes across instantly like a shutter coming down. It is always sudden and, for me at least, without any warning. It is usually the result of some small trigger (see C in **Figure 1**), a comment, act or omission that gets taken the wrong way. An interpretation is put onto something by me that causes me to react badly when otherwise I would laugh or simply ignore it. But the filter comes down immediately and once it is there I see the world through this greyness.

Figure 1: Stages of Depression.

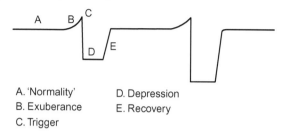

A. 'Normality'   D. Depression
B. Exuberance   E. Recovery
C. Trigger

In truth there probably is a build up to my depression. It takes time to come on and there may be signs. But I can never see it coming and it always takes me unawares. Sometimes those around me, who know me well, can spot the signs. It is usually an excess of exuberant behaviour or over-heightened emotions (see B in **Figure 1**).

This simple diagram, which is not to any scale and may well be too schematic, shows that the fall into depression is an iterative process. The periods between depressive episodes differ, as does the depth of the trough I fall into. But there is a pattern here. Indeed, it may be the case that this cycle should fit within a larger wave, in that I appear to have frequent bouts of depression and then periods when I appear less susceptible.

What is interesting is that the recovery is almost as immediate as the trigger into depression. I continue with the feeling that the world is against me and then, all of a sudden, as if by revelation, I come to realise that it isn't, or that there are greater priorities than my own feelings, like the welfare of my wife and family.

This diagram is what I have been able to put together by hindsight and by discussion with others who have observed the patterns of my behaviour. It is not something that has been obvious to me and, having described it, I am no more certain that I will be able to spot the signs in advance. I do not know either if what I have described here is distinctive or unique, or whether this pattern is typical of most or all depressives.

§

Depression is where the volume gets turned up high, where the intensity goes up. This might mean that depression is not something that only some people have, but rather it is a problem of controlling the intensity of certain feeling that we all have. For the depressive these feelings become more intense, they get out of control, and they take over, drowning out any other sounds including cries for help. All of us have self-esteem issues, doubts and worries, but most of the time and in most individuals, these are under control and do not take over the person. The illness, which I insist is not contagious, is not one of particular moods but the intensity and violence of their swings.

The idea that it might be a matter of intensity or volume helps us understand that filters need not be uniform in their intensity. They can have more or less effect. They have a variety of settings, such that, when the volume is very low, we might not even notice there is anything there at all.

§

A complication, which muddies the model of depression I have presented (Figure 1), is that I find I can slip in and out of depression: the volume, as it were, can be adjusted. I can be at home sulking or angry when a work colleague rings me. I will then speak to them entirely pleasantly and deal with the issues in my normal way. I may even joke with them. But as soon as I put the phone down the sulk comes back: the filter comes down again. Those in the house with me, who have borne the brunt of my depression, find this inexplicable. Those on the phone probably have no idea of any problems with depression at all. Again I don't know if this is common or unique: I presume it is the former.

This though is very unfair on those closest to me. They are the only ones who see me depressed and who have to contend with it. Is this a safety valve; that I know subconsciously that some people will deal with my depression with patience, empathy and love while others, who know me a good deal less well, might not? But if so, this sounds almost cynical.

What this suggests though is that depression is context dependent; otherwise I could not slip in and out of it apparently so readily. I am hardly ever, if at all, depressed or anxious outside my dwelling. It never occurs outside my home, and, whether this be symptom or cause, it is almost always triggered by someone who really matters to me. On one level this might be expected, in that I seldom feel like venturing out when I am depressed. But this is not the whole story as the example of phone calls from work shows. I can respond quite normally to colleagues and to complete strangers but not to my family, those who I love and who I am committed to. Is it really just because, despite my love for them, I intuit that I have far greater leeway? They will stick by me, whereas if I did the same things at work I would be sacked? This may be so, but I certainly do not consider this at the time. What is lacking in depression, despite any impressions to the contrary, is any calculation. Any act or comment is simply a reaction against something made on the spur of the moment.

But this suggests, as does the suddenness of its triggering and recovery, there must be some sort of switch to depression. It also suggests that this switch is not at the point of triggering (C in **Figure 1**) — by this time it is too late — but at the onset of exuberance (B in **Figure 1**). It is at this point that things start.

§

Anxiety and depression seems to be very good at controlling us, of hiding their workings-out, the mechanisms that they use to control us. It is like a magic trick where the hands move too quickly for us to follow, or where we are distracted and so lose track of what is happening. We think we know what is happening, that we have followed the moves, but we always lose, we never choose right. And this is because the trick is rigged. It is not a fair contest — it is not simply choosing one of three cups. The whole point of the show is to trick us, to bend reality. But in this case we are being conned by a very clever artist inside our head. This artist is very good at making one thing look like something else. And we are the willing dupes, putting our money down in the hope that this time we will choose right. What is worse is that we never learn. After all, the artist is in our head, and so we think it is us doing the trick. As a result we refuse to disbelieve our senses and take the magician for what he really is, namely, a con artist out to trick us of our sanity.

An important element in understanding what is going on here is to accept that the anxiety *is not who we are*. It is not part of us, or rather that is not what we are or need be. It is not part of my will but an alien force that is seeking to trick me. In this way we can try to separate ourselves from the anxiety and to see it as threat, as an outsider, rather than the trusted confidant it sets itself up to be. The virtue of this approach, which comes from Emanuel Swedenborg and his interpreters,[4] is that we begin to see the process, the workings out. We see that there is actually something happening here that is not part of our normal mental landscape. It helps us to differentiate between health and illness, between light and dark and between what helps us and what hinders. It forces us to notice the bad as alien and different rather than seeing it merely as part of what is always there. Splitting up the actions of our heads into two opposing places — what

Swedenborg called Heaven and Hell — allows us to differentiate and make active choices. It makes us notice that there is something going on and that it might be caused by something that does not have our best intentions at heart.

§

Depression is about feelings, often very raw ones, and there is little analysis going on. I just am. But this writing is an attempt at an analysis of depression. By definition I can only write when I am not depressed. Yet, because the chasm between my optimistic and depressed selves is so wide, it is very hard to actually reach what the feelings of depression are like. I cannot write or think clearly when depressed and so if I wish to look at it I can only do so with hindsight and try to understand it, if not quite from the outside, then at a little distance. I am therefore seeking to recreate my feelings and explain something about them.

What I find hardest to capture is the stasis of depression. It might be best to show this as a blank sheet of grey. This is a feeling of nothingness, where there is nothing to do, nothing I can settle on, where nothing suits. I feel uncomfortable, unsettled, but cannot pick anything to assuage this. No book, no film, I don't want a walk or to talk to anyone. There is often a sort of prickliness, an unease, a sense of itchy discomfort. I do not want to move, but I also want to do something and feel uneasy because I am doing nothing. On occasion I can turn to a comfort book or film, something I know well in terms of its emotional register, and this will help the moment pass. At other times all I can do is try to sleep it off, to close down and hope that it goes away.

§

One aspect of depression is repetition, of things repeating in my head on a loop. This stuff is often banal and meaningless, a series of disconnected words, often profane that I mumble or let run through my head. There is no attempt to make sense of anything, to deal with any issue, but just perhaps to vent something, to let off steam, to take out an imagined slight on the world in general. So I repeat a mantra to myself endlessly. It is like having a conspiracy with myself, and so it only offers a false comfort — because, as always, there is no conspiracy.

§

I am aware that my depression is only mild and that many suffer far worse than I have. I have never been hospitalised, my medication is relatively mild, and I have not had serious suicidal thoughts. Indeed, I have always thought suicide to be an immensely selfish act, which, I suppose, shows that I can still focus on others rather than being completed lost in my own head. Some parts of my life appear to be quite normal, even as I am more volatile and unpredictable than I once was. Having said all this, I also know that my depression has affected others as well as myself.

It does appear then that my condition is liveable with. I can survive as I am most of the time. I maintain a relatively normal life, at least outwardly. But while I am grateful for this, I also know that the downside of my depression not being so serious is that I have not had access to certain treatments that might have helped me. It is a comfort on one level to be assessed as not ill enough to be referred to a consultant psychologist, but this does not mean that I am completely well. It rather means I get nothing at all. I am not bitter about this and I know that scarce resources have to be rationed, but it does leave me with the perverse thought that if only my depression was worse I could get it sorted out. Of course, I don't seriously mean this: the depression seems bad enough at the time and I don't feel I need to imagine what it would be like if it were worse.

§

Am I falling into a bit of a trap here? Depression is where we internalise everything and focus on 'me'. But is not this work here doing precisely the same: it is all about me?

This may be the case, but how could I write authentically about depression in any other manner? If I wish to draw out the nature of the space inside my head, and if it really is as distinct and separate a space as I take it to be, then what other approach is there? Would it be better if I told this to someone else who then wrote it down and interpreted it based on their priorities? We might suggest that it depends on what those priorities were and how skilled an interpreter this person was. But would the supposed objectivity of an independent observer help here, or would it hinder? What would be the benefit of more distance, more interpretation and mediation? Would it not actually become less real? I would suggest that it is subjectivity that makes the writing real and authentic here, even if it does need some allowance to be made for personal preoccupations (but why would an interpreter not have their personal preoccupations too?).

I do not feel I can write about someone else's feelings in an authentic manner. I can only attempt to encapsulate my own thoughts and feelings, and I can only do this once I am free of depression myself. This though is very hard work and has only been possible after some intense therapy sessions and a lot of pushing. This has involved trawling back — something I actively try not to do — and so seeking a better understanding of places I am currently very glad to be very far away from.

In any case, this work is not just about my depression, but a more general consideration of our most private space. However, the nature of our private thoughts is such that we can only do this through one set of lived experiences. In this way we can see the range of emotions and feelings and the nature of our headspace as a very private, yet also largely unknown, dark and uncontrollable space.

§

If we keep our mouth shut no one can get to know our thoughts. We really do not need to give up our secrets. We might be the victim of force and so feel we have to speak. We could be tortured to reveal our secrets, but this is a notoriously ineffective means of information gathering. There is no guarantee that what the victim cries out is true. And of course, for most of us, most of the time, we are not under duress of any kind. We are seldom deemed important enough to be tortured to reveal our inner most thoughts.

Inside our head is where we are really by ourselves. It is where we are truly alone with our thoughts. No one else can find them and gain access to them but us. Anyone outside has to go through us and with our co-operation. We can deny or limit access, and we always do. There is always more in there than we will ever let out. We know this because we all dissemble when it suits us: we hold things back, we say one thing when we mean another, we speak obliquely, or we just keep quiet. There is nothing to stop us doing this and often nothing particularly wrong in us doing so. No crime is committed in most cases, all we are doing is being circumspect and so we protect ourselves and perhaps others too. Our dissembling is most often harmless. We are merely sifting and filtering our thoughts, choosing what we offer to others, knowing everyone else does the same. Indeed an excess of candour is often unwanted and unwelcome. We want others to be circumspect and diplomatic in what they say and do. We deploy good manners and insist on civilised standards to protect others and ourselves, and we stay within conventions for the same reason. Much of what is in within our head is not for popular consumption. It needs to be edited, processed and to be thought through.

To be thoughtful does not mean that we have many thoughts, but that we are considerate in how we use those we have.

§

Our headspace can be a cluttered and ill-disciplined place. It has the informality of a place that we need never show to anyone else. It is a completely private space that no else will see. Indeed, there are parts — the unconscious bits — that we ourselves do not see much of either. But the fact that we do not have visitors alters how we use the space, where we leave things, if and when we tidy up, whether we turn things off properly or not. Our bad habits go uncorrected and our slipshod methods remain unobserved and so unimproved. And, there is a lot of space — it appears almost infinite — so we can hide things away.

§

Psychoanalysts claim that they can read our dreams and so tell us something about our unconscious motives and urges. But to do this they have had to develop a standardised lexicon of meanings and the only means that they been able to do this is through the interpretation of dreams; that is the very things they are seeking to interpret. Indeed as the title of perhaps Freud's most famous book suggests, the key word here is 'interpretation'.[5] Freud does not really know what we are thinking. What he has done rather is to apply a preconceived set of ideas of his own to the reports that others have given him of their dreams. He has interpreted the mediated concepts of others as a means of allowing him to interpret the mediated concepts of yet others. So Freud's method is based on the conceit that he can see into the minds of his patients based on their descriptions of their recollected dreams. But he can only do this based on what has been recollected, or rather what has been said to him about these recollections. The process is thoroughly mediated by the facility his patients have with language to convert their dreams into a common mode of speech that can be so standardised as to allow for comparisons. The method depends on an exactness of language that simply cannot be guaranteed. How does Freud know that his patients are describing precisely the same thing when they apparently use the same word? And this is before we get to how Freud uses his preconceptions to develop an interpretation.

§

What I am interested in here is the subjectivity of our headspace — as a space for thinking, feeling and the emotions. It is not a literal space, yet there seems to be no limits to what it can store: no file is too big and we can just keep on adding more and more memories. All of these are only accessible to the one person, who can choose to share them provided, of course, they are capable of successfully transferring the correct meaning to others.

We cannot read the thoughts of another. We can read their letters, their emails, their diaries, we can hear their confessions, but we cannot get to the raw thoughts behind these expressions of a person.

How well do we know our own head? Do we know it as well as where we live or work? We cannot see it, and we do not really sense it at all. If we opened the space up there would not actually be any space: It is full of organic matter and appears to have little to do with thoughts, feelings and emotions.

So we would struggle to describe what is inside our heads: how big it is in there, what shape it is and so on. We do not know how heavily populated this space is: Is it full of thoughts and memories, or are there open spaces waiting to be filled? Where are things stored away? We are coming up here against metaphor: there is, properly speaking, no headspace. It is full of brain, a massively complex and only partially understood organic structure. No one has found the mind, never mind the soul, and there does not appear to be a filing system or databank. It is not then a space that we can actively explore.

Yet there is so much going on in there. Whole empires of thoughts, memories, arguments, complete monologues, movies in full colour, countless buildings we can walk through, dreams and imagining of things that have never, and perhaps can never, exist. There are whole civilisations in there that no one else can know and we are unable to catalogue it all even if we could access it all. What is inside need bear no relation to what is outside and it need not be mirrored in our speech and actions.

And much of this goes on without our conscious control. We do not decide when and what we dream; we cannot decide what we forget or remember; we cannot control our mood swings; we develop prejudices and preconceptions without really wishing to and we change our minds — we go from believing one thing to believing the opposite; and we get angry. We have some control over all this and we can train ourselves to get better at it. We can train our memory and our brains to develop differently according to how they engage with technologies and with others. We can learn in different ways: medieval monks relied on rote learning and memory recall, while a modern scholar retrieves the same information from the Internet. But however we develop our capacities, the control that we have remains limited and we cannot order our headspace just how we would like it to be.

§

I can look at a mirror and see into my eyes. I can look at my hands, feet, stomach, but I cannot see my headspace. So I cannot see the most intimate part of me, the bit that no one else can gain access to. Of course, I cannot see my heart or my liver, but these, as essential as they are, do not communicate and tell me things. Part of the issue, and this does apply to all the major organs too, is that what goes on in my head is unconscious in the sense that it does not need my active knowledge. I breathe without asking my lungs to do it each time, and likewise unwanted thoughts come together and I dream. Much of the mechanisms in my head run automatically, as programs in the background. But unlike my breathing what comes into my head has no regularity or predictability. I can't simply take what comes for granted.

§

Depression means we cannot help but question our own competence. One of the worst things about depression is that we start to view ourselves how we think others might actually see us. We feel that the blinkers have come off and we are no longer capable of deluding others. But all of this is without the slightest bit of evidence, other than the manner in which we interpret the responses of others to our actions. How people react might not be quite what we thought they ought to be and so we start to wonder what they really do feel. But, in reality, these reactions are exactly how people have always responded to us. Nothing has really changed for them. What is different now is the ontological fragility, caused by depression, that does not allow us to ignore the inconsequential, but rather inflates it to something of enormous significance.

Anxiety is where we doubt another's motives without any reason other than that we can no longer trust our own.

§

Do our thoughts gang up on us? Can they conspire against us? Are they necessarily on our side? Does it make sense to talk about 'sides' in this regard? Can we properly fight against ourselves? Or is this completely the wrong metaphor? Should we really be thinking of fighting our thoughts? But if not, does this mean then that we would have to give in to those thoughts that seem to be bringing us down? What does 'giving in' to one's thoughts mean anyway? Is it just taking up one thought against another: we accept one and reject another? We know that our thoughts can contradict each other, that they can oppose each other.

There are lots of questions here, and all too few answers. But what we do know is that we cannot dispense with our thoughts, with thinking itself. 'I could dispense with my thoughts' is after all a thought. So, and this means more questions, can we ever not think? Is to be awake to be thinking?

§

Changing direction in the way we live is difficult. We may make resolutions, we may appear determined to change, but often these are short-lived. Certain ways of behaving are so ingrained and resonate so fully with how we live and think that they are hard to break free of. Quite often these established ways are so because they are enjoyable, even, or especially, the bad habits, and we have grown used to them so that we do not notice we are doing them. It is this aspect — the transparency, the taken-for-granted ordinariness — that makes any change so difficult to achieve and to maintain. It is often difficult to keep in a new direction when we are 'trained' to go in another. Under pressure or when we are busy, without thinking we will revert back to the default mode. Also changing one habit will often mean changing others. If we try to give up smoking we might also find it hard to drink, or to meet up with certain friends who are smokers and might encourage us to light up. We might have a drink of an evening to relax, and so if we really want to relax, why not just have the one cigarette? So to change one habit may mean altering others and so the cost becomes much higher. The consequences of the change start to escalate and there may become a choice between which habit is most important. Perhaps we want to maintain the friendship of a smoker more than giving up the habit ourselves or we think that giving up drinking is too hard and so we keep on smoking as well.

But, at different times, the balance of these habits changes, and the relative costs alter. So a person who failed to give up smoking many times may finally succeed and never smokes again. Or it might be that someone gives up and does not smoke for many years, but then they begin again because of a particular incident or when their will is weakened. All this, of course, is well known and well documented.[6] Yet it becomes no more predictable as a result. We are dealing here at the limits of rational behaviour, where weakness of will, addiction and purposive choice all interact, as Jon Elster has argued at length. The particular life history and psychology of individuals make it hard to state that a person in a given situation will respond in a particular manner. All we have, as Elster concedes, are mechanisms that help us to understand how a situation may have come about. These mechanisms are not predictive or necessary, but are explicable on a *post factum* basis only. Elster states that in trying to understand a person's attitude to alcohol we can look to their parent's behaviour as an explanatory mechanism. The child may be reacting against alcoholic parents, or has been brought up in a teetotal household: either version could help us explain the child's aversion to alcohol, but without providing any sense of direct causality. The important limit here is the inability to generalise from any specific case (as in the case above, one could be a teetotaller for one of two quite opposite reasons).

Elster in his discussion on rational choice considers the impact that beliefs, information sets and weakness or strength of will have on a person's incentive structures. How are incentives towards or against an action altered and conditioned by information, by belief, but also by a propensity towards addiction? If these alter then this will change the incentive structure and make an act more or less likely.

What we can factor into this is the manner in which somebody is able to insulate their incentives, to hide away from others. If someone is able to protect their beliefs, and is not open to new information, then they can retain a stable incentive structure even where this is harmful. We can characterise insulation as where one is not open to the new and the different and thus able to maintain stability in beliefs and action. We might see this as an act of will, as a deliberate act. So a refusal to change is not due to a blithe ignorance, but is actually a wilful refusal to come to terms with something; it is a deliberate holding off of a situation. We might even suggest that given their particular circumstances they perceive a very short time horizon, which is determined by the ability to get past another day without facing a challenge.

However, the day may dawn when insulation is no longer tenable. We are faced with a new set of information and come to realise that we can no longer hide away from our problems. We have reached the limits of our wilfulness, and now we face a new challenge, and so accordingly our beliefs need to change. Our belief that we could get away with the issue is no longer tenable and so we are now faced with a new set of circumstances based on this recognition that some action now has to be taken. It now becomes rational to act differently and towards a different aim. It is no longer possible for us to hold onto the pretence that there is no problem. What this shows is Elster's insistence that rational decision-making depends on beliefs as well as information. If we believe we will not get caught, and if our past experience shows this to be well founded, then we are behaving quite rationally to act accordingly.

What this suggests is that if we insulate ourselves properly from external influences we can be said to be acting rationally no matter how skewed our beliefs are. The issue is whether it would be reasonable to assert that we could have believed something different. This leads us to suggest that one person's sense of rationality might differ quite markedly from another's: the insulated person sees an issue completely differently from the external spectator. Both views, we must admit, are partial, but are based on different sets of justified beliefs.

Of course, it also shows that we can make a case for bizarre actions being determined as rational! If one can properly assert that their beliefs are well established then it is indeed rational. Most of us consider that our beliefs are well founded and based on sensible and rational suppositions. This may be absurd or indeed ill founded, but it is only in hindsight that we would have much of an opportunity to come to this conclusion. Most of us believe we act with good reason and seek to proceed in this manner. Whether it meets external criteria is perhaps not relevant.

§

Responsibility becomes more onerous the longer we have been free of it: it weighs heavier because of the lightness of our existence without it. Perhaps this explains how we slide into solitude: it might start as something temporary — a rejection from a lover, or a reaction to loss or grief — but once it has begun, and we find that there is some relief in the silence and lack of others, we begin to relish it and fear a return to our former life. As a result we lose contact with friends and family, find reasons not to interact and so we get forgotten and our solitude gets locked in. Perhaps this then leads to a fear of contact, because we are no longer used to it, or because we fear that it may bring with it the unpredictable and what we might struggle to control. Søren Kierkegaard talks of 'an internal consistency', so that the drunk fears the consequences of being sober, and the demonic person has the fear of 'someone stronger in the good'. The demonic person is fearful because, as he has this internal consistency, he 'has a totality to lose'. Only by continuing fully

on this path can he remain unweakened. To face our opposite, to have our way challenged is therefore to disturb ourselves, to weaken the totality of our view. So, as Kierkegaard
points out, the sinful person is held together by their sin.
Thus this internal consistency, the completeness of our life,
perpetuates what from the outside might be seen as harmful
behaviour. Our behaviour feeds on itself, growing more and
more as we rely upon it and refuse to have it challenged. It is
all too easy to retain the established patterns, and much
harder to envisage or even tackle an alternative that challenges these presumptions. We believe that we have no reason
to challenge ourselves because we feel whole, and, in the case
of solitude, there is no one around to do the challenging. We
can therefore convince ourselves that we are doing nothing
wrong simply because we are never told that we are, and we
simply refuse to put ourselves into a position of being
challenged.

§

There is no logic to anxiety and perhaps it would be wrong
to seek any in it. To be logical, rational and reasonable about
our anxiety is to have controlled it and thus to have defeated
it, at least for a time. But when we are depressed, how could
the world ever be any different?

§

Once anxiety starts, once it takes hold of us, we cannot easily
rid ourselves of it. This is because it forms what we may see
as a moving target. It may start as a result of a particular loss
or fear of loss, but it soon develops, or spreads into a more
generalised sense, and it soon attaches itself to other issues,
other fears and problems, it levers its way in and widens that
crack until it gapes. Using another metaphor, it magnifies the
dilemma, turning the minor to the major, the small into the
large. And we find that we can no longer deal with this issue

as we might have done before, we can no longer treat it in proportion.

So anxiety may move, it can travel, but we, as a result, do not. Anxiety creates stasis and we become immobile and unable to act. We lack motivation, incentives and any urge to move. Instead we turn in on ourselves and we look inwards instead of outwards. What is internal to us — our worries, concerns and problems — take over and this is all we can care about. We are tied up from the inside with this tense knot of anxiety, a tension coiling inside us.

§

Anxiety wastes time. Having no motivation, we do nothing. We stare into space; we try to sleep; we cling to ourselves in a darkened room. We can do nothing more than this as the anxiety takes over and immobilises us. This is why the dwelling, and its apparently unchanging nature, is so important to the anxious person. The dwelling encloses us whilst anxiety gnaws at us from the inside. This does not mean we need dwelling to be anxious — it is not a condition of anxiety — but rather dwelling makes anxiety survivable.

§

What is the range of anxiety? Does it include the squeaking door we know we ought to mend but haven't, or the dripping tap we have neglected?

§

We wish to eliminate transience and uncertainty, even as we operate within it. We want the benefits that choice, openness and change bring with them and what potential they can offer us, but we do not wish the flux and the risk that inevitably comes as well. Hence our anxiety, manifested in our concern of not being able to cope, in our belief that we need to cope, and desire of wanting to cope, but fearing we will fail.

§

We want to use our dwelling to display ourselves, to tell other people about us, to compete, to strut, to show off. But we also want to use it to hide us away from the world, which pressures us, places demands upon us and forces us into routines, patterns and typologies not of our own choosing. We do not want to be beholden to the expectations of others, even as we play up to them with our displays. We want our dwelling to both perform and protect, to show us off and to hide us.

§

One of the virtues of our private dwelling, where we are enclosed and can exclude others, is that we feel we have less, or even no, need to be responsible. We can operate without any sense of being beholden to others, and we need not relate to anything other than ourselves and perhaps those closest to us. We might suppose, quite properly, that this state is, in a way, reprehensible. We might be encouraged to feel that we should show solidarity to others. We should take responsibility for others beyond the immediate circle of our family and friends, as well as standing up for ourselves (responsibility in the sense of being independent). Yet being in this state of enclosure, where we feel free from others, is a necessary one. It need not be the permanent state or the default position. We do not have to be apart always from others and to completely ignore the world. But the very state of being enclosed is what makes sharing and the care for others possible. It is because we can be enclosed that we can share, support others and care for them. In private dwelling we can be free of wider responsibilities and this allows us to stop, look around and focus, and what our gaze alights upon is those we love.

But there is more to the enclosure provided by private dwelling. Having the security, comfort and complacency of this place means we have a base from which to venture outwards. We can do this precisely because we know we have a place that we can return to. And when we wish to we can take others into our enclosure and offer them a kind of support and care that we could not provide in any public space.

But how does this need for security and to be free from responsibility operate for the anxious and the depressed? When a person becomes, because of depression, so insular and focused on the inward sense of their self rather than any notion of being together, we can then see how this need to be free from responsibility loses any sense of proportion and becomes not a possibility but the principal form of relief. This flight from responsibility might be seen to take over completely and become the single most important state. The anxiety we feel magnifies the onerous nature of responsibility and negates any sense of the solidarity we gain from togetherness.

§

Anxiety is not a concern for what others might think or say about us. It replaces care with indifference. We do not, or cannot, factor others into our situation. Instead we look only inwards, and are consumed by this insularity. Accordingly, we can say that anxiety isolates us, it cuts us off from others because they cannot share our fears, they do not understand nor share our lack of proportion. Others cannot see the world as we do, and our anxiety makes us suspicious of them for this lack of insight.

Or at least this is what we think. We believe there to be this gulf, this separation between us and others, which our sense of isolation discourages us from questioning or seeking to contest. Our anxiety is the chief provider *and* proof of our suspicions.

§

How can we get rid of our anxiety? We might try to face up to our fears. But if anxiety comes from within, and if it is general and non-specific, how can we face up to it? What should we be looking at?

We might try to keep busy, so we have no time to dwell on our anxieties. But what incentive do we have to try? Where is there to go? Are we not better hiding? Is this not the best way to avoid our anxieties?

What help can we expect here from dwelling? Does it help or hinder us? Might not the privacy and security we seek from dwelling turn us towards indolence? And might not this be because of the very things we seek from our dwelling? Our dwelling, we think, is always something we can rely on and take comfort from, as well as being comfortable in. So might we then see it as where we are, so to speak, *safe* in our anxiety? Could we not see our dwelling in this sense as acting like the proverbial padded cell, which prevents us from harming ourselves and doing damage to others? Our dwelling is the place we do not need to venture out of. It is where we are free to be, where we can ignore others, and do not have to face up to those things we would rather avoid. And around us always is this sense of certainty — the padding, as it were — provided us by dwelling.

Anxiety causes us to retreat, and we need some place where we can go, where we can find solace because other people, who do not feel how we feel, can never assuage our uneasiness. Our dwelling is one such retreat, and perhaps it is the main one, in that only through dwelling can we fully hide away. Whereas in public we might feel exposed or naked, in private we are covered up, clothed and therefore we feel protected. And, yes, this is indeed very much akin to crawling under a stone, or withdrawing into our shell. But isn't this precisely what we need, or rather what we feel we need, as the knot tightens in our stomach and we lose any sense of proportion? We can be safe; we feel we are safe. Our anxieties may still hold us, but there are no expectations on us, no responsibilities and no one to chide us.

In this way, is anxiety not the ultimate in nihilism: blankness, the opposing of anything and everything?

§

There is something determinedly misanthropic in anxiety. It brings out the worst of us, and makes it hard to find anything in others that we might wish to redeem. But, and I am not sure if I really mean this, might not a (presumably carefully controlled) dose of misanthropy actually be healthy for us? Might it not help us to realise that imperfection, failure, embarrassment and disappointment are much more the norm than the isolated depressive might otherwise think, and accordingly we might realise that we should not expect so much of ourselves or from others.

§

Anxiety cuts us off from achieving anything else. We turn away from the future and remain focused on the terminus of the present and the fractures of the past. Hence we tend to dwell on things that embarrass us, those things we regret doing long in our past. Anxiety is the feeling that we ought to have done or should do something different, whilst knowing full well it is now too late.

§

Anxiety offers merely the illusion of freedom. It feels like an early release from responsibility, and we are relieved that we do not have to care. To be alone and to be able to concern ourselves with our thoughts and only our thoughts is the aim, and the possibility of achieving this freedom is the fiction the depressed live by, where we can unload all responsibility and withdraw into the sanctity of our dwelling and be alone. But achieving this is seldom possible, and we find this frustrating. Having said this, its achievement too would be self-defeating, the very termination of all possibility.

In any case, all we can do is delay the onset of responsibility. We still owe the debt, so to speak, and all the time the interest is piling up, and the problem is getting worse. So when we cannot avoid it any longer and we have to face it, the problem is now larger and more complex, while we are now even less capable of dealing with it. We perhaps know this, can take it in and accept it when we are told. We know that we should act and deal with what we know we are merely putting off. But this knowledge really does not help us, and it does not make it any easier for us to face it in the here and now. As long as the problem can be put in another place, we will do so.

Perhaps in time we realise just how unfree we are. The burden still lurks just out of sight, but not totally out of our consciousness, and we know we will need to face it sometime and somewhere. Yet we still put it off and pretend we feel better for it.

§

If one of the key problems of depression is that we do not realise the extent of our problem, how can we solve it? We are often told that the first stage in getting better is to realise the scale of the problem, and therefore see the need to get help. However, with depression, the issue is precisely that we will not face our problems.

That we live in private space plays a big part in this. When dwelling works well it is what prevents us from realising the full scale of our problems. Dwelling cushions us, allows us to hide our problems from others. We feel we are safe and so we ourselves can hide from our problems and refuse to see them. The door we can lock appears to keep the problem out. We use the implacability of dwelling to maintain our delusions.

We cannot expect dwelling to change or improve us. It remains passive to our actions. Dwelling, after all, is but a tool, and this means it can work for good or ill, for us or against us. Dwelling in this way merely magnifies a problem or a virtue. The routines of dwelling can help us by creating a virtuous circle, reinforcing our relations with others through their reiteration. But, if we are alone, we remain alone, and dwelling can make our isolation more complete.

There is no inevitability here. How dwelling works for us depends on circumstance. Dwelling can help us. But it is necessary as background, as the stage upon which we act. It is not the foreground of our lives. Our dwelling does not provide the script, determine the action, and nor is it able to interpret what we have done. It can help us to focus down on to things, to emphasise them, and it can help us to avoid others. But it does not create them and will not necessarily solve them.

§

Is anxiety a result of having our illusions questioned by others, or by certain incidents, so that we cannot avoid looking closely and critically at ourselves? We look inwards and call into question all we have done, all we have believed, all we have held close to us, all those certainties, aspirations and dreams. Once our illusions are shattered, once we find we cannot rely on this self-image we have fought so hard to establish, what have we left? We are, in a sense, spiritually naked, our ontological security now stripped away. Part of this disillusioning may be a result of ageing, of a realisation, which we can no longer avoid, that we are not destined to achieve what we had hoped, what we thought would one day be in our grasp. Those things, be they in our personal life or career, which we thought would arrive, and which we relied on, took comfort in, are now seen to be nothing but naïveté, nothing but a chimera, the fool's gold of an optimistic and rash sense of certainty. And now we have to come to terms with this world without illusions, this emptier, colder, perhaps even crueller world, in which we are more insignificant than we had thought.

Perhaps at the root of anxiety is the realisation that, after all and despite what we had hoped and even expected, nothing is ever going to change, and this place where we now are is as good as it will ever get. So the anger we might find welling up at times is really at ourselves, at the reality of what we are and that we can no longer sustain the illusion of what we thought we could be. It now dawns on us, that we are not as good as we thought we were, we will never be as successful, not as rich, not as lucky, not as clever, not even as good a person as we thought we were, that we will not now meet our expectations. And what makes this even worse for us is that the only one we can blame for this, the only real cause, is ourselves, whether it be our failings or even our very expectations themselves.

So we might see anxiety as about coming to terms with the limits of our uniqueness, that we can do only so much, that what future we have is not open, that many routes are cut off, many options are voided, and that we ourselves are finite, and now we know it.

§

Anxiety brings with it a sense of indecision, and we may as a result appear indifferent to others and the world generally. Indeed this may not be an act and we actually are indifferent. We have no time to consider others because of the worry, pain and concerns that envelop us. We are sealed up whilst we traverse through the world, ignoring others, but feeling and believing that we are the ones being ignored. Anxiety cuts us off from others so that we are unable to share with them and connect with them. Any association with others is dominated by our anxiety and we see others and the world around us through this distorting lens.

§

Why would we ever be anxious in our own dwelling, the place that we know best? It is a space where we can relax and be calm. It is predictable and does not tend to change and so we can rely on it. But, if we wish we can change it to our tastes. We know it intimately and, generally speaking, it is under our control. It is the only place where we feel we are in control, it being explicitly made by and for us. We are able to separate ourselves from those situations that may create or magnify anxiety. We are close to those we can love and trust: we can choose whom we share with and who we are close to. In this way, we might think, that dwelling can assuage our anxieties. It is where we need not extend ourselves or go beyond what we know and are comfortable with. It makes no demands on us, but rather we can rely on it. Dwelling can be a crutch and support.

But when we are anxious, we also might not feel any close association with our dwelling, and this is precisely because our anxiety isolates us from things as well as people. So we do not reciprocate the dwelling's support and assistance to us. We feel a sense of ambivalence towards our own dwelling as a result of our anxiety. Hence we might not actively maintain it, improve it or change it (and certainly not move to another better one). We want it to be there, but not to have to focus on it, to have it anywhere near the centre of our thoughts. Indeed we have nothing, and perhaps want nothing, to be at the centre of our thoughts other than our anxiety; or perhaps more accurately, we should state this negatively and say that the current focus of our anxiety — the journey, the meeting, the person — looms so large that nothing else can enter in, there is simply no space for anything or anyone else, even as we continue, without any acknowledgement, to rely on some things and some people to help us through our anxiety.

Dwelling can then help us in our anxiety, but anxiety is in no way supportive of dwelling. Dwelling means we can flourish, but anxiety does not help dwelling to thrive. It is parasitic on dwelling, as it is of much else besides. Anxiety eats away at us and gives us nothing back. Properly speaking, there is no relationship with anxiety, no reciprocity, merely a one-sided deal in which anxiety is the winner and so able to take all there is. In this manner we can say that anxiety is always destructive of our health, our relationships and of our dwelling.

This means that there is only so long that we can live with anxiety. Of course, there is no exact time, no prescribed length, and no specific level of severity after which anxiety becomes unsupportable. But there is still a limit, after which everything is lost.

§

One thing that anxiety cannot deal with is change. We know that things will change, that it is inevitable and that we are powerless to stop it. But we dread it. We cannot predict the results of change, but we know that we cannot really avoid them. We cannot stop change, and know that it is futile to try. Yet much of what we hold dear is threatened by change. This may lead us to a form of fatalism, a grim acceptance that we cannot protect what is important to us, and so why should we try. Or it might elicit anger in us, over what we have lost, or will lose, and so we might fight against it, throw ourselves against the agents of change, even though we know it may well be futile. Or we might just have a quiet anxiety, an uneasiness that insinuates itself into our brains and makes it hard for us to feel comfortable. We have this sense that something is about to happen. It may be inchoate, unformed and imprecise, yet we still have a sense of unease. Of course, nothing may happen, but this does not assuage us. It is always still about to come. Change need not actually materialise for us to worry over it. Indeed what worries us is precisely the prospect of change, the belief in the inevitability of change and our powerlessness in the face of it. The issue is partly one of scale, of one individual against the world, of an inability to push back the tide and prevent the flow from picking us up and carrying us away. Yet perversely, this is a feeling that comes from the inside, from us, and which we, despite our best efforts to remain rational, attach to these external things that we feign not to understand. I say feign, because at other times, at our most lucid and out-going, we can place ourselves and gain a proper sense of proportion.

It is here that we can see the significance of dwelling: in its implacability as a tool that helps us to connect or that assists us in building a fortress of anxiety against the world. The dwelling can protect us and keep us safe, as well as the place of comfort and connection with our loved ones. But is also the stone to hide under, where we can cower in fear, and withdraw from those necessary connections that bring with them perspective and proportion.

§

The conditions of change are of anxiety and ambivalence. On the one hand, we fear change, we seek to hold onto what we have and know and we may come to resent what threatens to alter us and our environment. We cannot face intrusion, the unknown and the unavailing. But, on the other hand, we implicitly accept change all around us. We fail to notice this as it is happening. The changes are often imperceptible, the drip-drip of tiny accretions, which might over time alter how we live and the manner in which we understand ourselves. We have considerable capabilities to assimilate new things. We are able to adapt and to make use of new tools and equipment and to adapt old ones to new uses, so that we can maintain ourselves how we want to be. And we use these new and adapted tools to resist the unrecognised and the unwanted. The result is that our anxiety is not diminished, but merely it begins to operate in a different manner. Not that we notice the difference precisely because of our ambivalence.

§

Our anxieties are not always manifest to ourselves, and we may not be aware of the impact that they have on us and on others. Indeed, our anxiety is the very thing that prevents us acknowledging these effects. We are simply not prepared, perhaps not even able, to look beyond ourselves.

§

We are always, in a banal sense, ourselves. Whatever we do, whatever changes we make, we cannot become other than ourselves. We may consider ourselves to be different subjects at different times, but we override this with a sense of continuity, a day-to-day, month-to-month, year-to-year narrative, in which we find ourselves centred on the present with reference to the past and with our hopes for the future. Anxiety arises, perhaps, from the sense of ourselves as fixed by the past in the present and how this clashes with our desire to change ourselves in the future.

§

Do we actively insulate ourselves, or is it something we just fall into? And do we actually notice what we are doing? Most of the changes we are prey to are small and so any movement is incremental, consisting only of very small moves or shifts that take us imperceptibly towards a more isolated and insular existence. Of course, there are some people who actively isolate themselves, who seek the hermit's life. But these people will perhaps always be few in number.

Yet we can argue that all acts are intentional, including acts of omission such as refusing to go out or to accept an invitation. The issue though is that the reason for the refusal will always be specific to the occasion rather than a grand design, or at least that is how it appears to us, and how we might seek to rationalise it to ourselves and to others. We are not prepared to see ourselves as ill or following a particular predictable pattern. However, if we can ever be persuaded to look at ourselves more honestly, we might see that we always find some reason to say, 'No, sorry, I can't come'. Something will always present itself to allow us to back out from the thing we don't wish to do.

But we try very hard not to be honest with ourselves and avoid situations where we are forced to look at ourselves with candour. In this way insulation becomes self-fulfilling, in that it dispenses with the need to look at ourselves honestly. So part of the desire for insulation is this refusal to look at ourselves, and therefore have to face the challenge of dealing with our problems. We do not want to face the issues and so we use any strategy to avoid having to do so. What this means is that insulation and withdrawal become ends in themselves, they become the very purpose of the act and the fact that one remains untroubled and unchallenged is suffi-cient justification to continue acting in that manner. There is here a circularity that reinforces the refusal to engage, and isolation then appears beneficial.

But might we not claim that there is indeed some advan-tage in separating ourselves? This may be a delusion, but might we not suggest that when we sit apart, when we take ourselves out of the world around us, we actually feel we can view it better and more clearly? We can determine more completely how the world is, because instead of being within it, amongst it and going with its flows and torrents, we are now sitting on the shore watching the activities of others. We are a dispassionate observer rather than an active player too busy to notice the flows as they occur.

Accordingly, what others might describe as isolation and solitude we would see as insulation. We are protecting ourselves from any infection from the outside world, so that we can sit at the margins, objectively observing human follies and silliness. We guardedly observe things through our part-closed curtains, we view what is happening while not being seen ourselves, and thus we see others as they are without the self-consciousness that comes from knowing they are being watched. The solitude then is a positive, intentional stepping-away from participation, allowing us to see things more clearly than others. Or at least this is what we might tell ourselves and want to believe.

We can question whether this manifests arrogance, cynicism or delusion; that we are 'better' than others, that we are a voyeur, or that we have a false view of the world and are wrong in believing that we have such a privileged insight. How can we tell if it is so, and if we are as cynical and as arrogant as it appears would we be bothered to find out? We might justifiably be wary of those who sit on the periphery and just look. We might wonder about their motives and what are they are trying to prove. It would be hard to see then as benign, and their very inscrutability and refusal to join in makes us wary of them.

This might lead us to suggest that to be isolated or fully insulated is to deny the possibility of empathy. By acting in this manner we prevent others from fully understanding our predicament, from seeing the world as we do, which is what is meant by empathy. We can feel sorry for a person, we can pity them, but we cannot feel as they do, at least not unless we are in the same situation. But being in the same situation is just what isolation does not permit. Empathy presumes engagement and involvement with another, yet this is precisely what the insulated person seeks to shirk. They neither want to be involved, nor for others to get involved with them.

The easiest thing for the person on the outside to do is precisely what the person inside wants of them: to ignore them, to give them no thought and so to walk on past. We see the door is closed and so walk on by. We do not see the person around or hear from them and so we forget them, or at least put them to the back of our minds as we get on with our own lives, concentrating instead on the easier contacts and less difficult situations. We take the least resistance and concentrate on what is before us. And so, unless the person is really close — a family member, partner, or close friend — we may well soon drift away from them. The insulated person may not even notice this, of course, because separating themselves off is the very state that they have explicitly or implicitly sought to achieve. They may on occasions regret not seeing someone but perhaps not, or not often enough, and they certainly do nothing about it, as they drift away into their self-imposed exile.

§

When we are depressed we fall back on our dwelling, on its *ur*-value, on its basic ontological framing as a source of protection. We find we have to rely more heavily on the intimacy that is protected by dwelling. And there is comfort in this. Yet the dwelling, and the protection it offers, can be diminished by our inability to reciprocate, so that the intimacy becomes one-sided, a half-life and starts to decay. When we are depressed the order and form brought by dwelling, as formatted by protected intimacy, is itself threatened. The withdrawal into dwelling by the depressed person threatens intimacy by its lack of reciprocity, by the inability to look across into the face of this very special other. We turn our gaze inwards.

The look of the depressive can be seen as one that does not really see anything at all. It is the unfocussed stare of one who eyes are open only incidentally, only open out of habit, in a fiction of seeing. The gaze instead is inwards, a scrolling down the soul, an inner process of scrutiny, or rather a random focussing on events and times, occasions of embarrassment, of regret, of missed opportunities, and of false and true endings.

In this way — through a concentration on the internal, the internal as concentrated — the dwelling and its protected intimacy becomes contingent upon the whim of this futile inward gaze. The dwelling becomes modelled by this longing, this loss, this regret, and becomes a harbourer of ghosts, the station of the transient. And this transience becomes magnified by the implacability of dwelling and casts its shadow — its taint — over intimacy and the relations on which it thrives. And our loved ones — looking on and trying to inspire us — find it hard to contend with our ghosts. They find it hard to deal with transient figures, with a troubled soul in motion.

We can picture protected intimacy,[7] and therefore the dwelling that surrounds it, by its imperturbability, by its stability, stasis and complacency, all a function of security. Yet when transience enters — when this intimacy begins to harbour ghosts, and ghosts that cannot be shared because they come from within, and are singular themselves — this stability is disturbed. The still waters are themselves troubled. And dwelling finds it hard to cope, hard to deal with, because it is built to deal with the external threat, to protect what is inside from what is outside. Yet now the threat is internal, it comes from within. The danger here is that the pressure built up from within cannot be naturally released. The strength of dwelling can absorb much, and the intimacy, the love, the stores of stability can likewise withhold much. But the walls are built to keep things out and to hold us safe within. What may happen then is a leakage — a failure of the insulation, an unnatural break in the fabric of dwelling. But this also breaks the intimacy, the security, the stability and things start to move, perhaps all too quickly, out of our control and things fall apart. Dwelling is easier to destroy from within, from those elements subversive of protected intimacy, those who undermine the security through the selfishness of the internal gaze, through the poison of anxious introspection with its cost, its betrayal of the intimacy and the love of others who we still must rely on.

It is for this reason, this consequence of insularity, that anxiety has to be faced and the reasons for it dealt with. In particular, we need to start looking outwards and to look into the face of the other. But we should not look just to anyone, but to those we should trust and who still trust us, those who can forgive much, who are prepared to share the consequences, the hard work of renewal, because they too are suffering, they too feel the weight of our ghosts.

What we need to rely on is the very resilience of dwelling itself, to trust it and those it seeks to protect, and to do this before it breaks under the strain of our indifference to it.

We should remember that while we have to maintain it, dwelling does not break in a day. It will give us some time and space in which to work ourselves back out again. It can teach us to exercise our voice again and to start to see others, and to see ourselves as we are seen, as we are, and not as we feel we are, or wish we are, or as we regret not being.

NOTES

1. Heidegger (1962).

2. Lachman (2013).

3. See for example Beck (1992), Porter and Dunant (1997) and Salecl (2004).

4. Swedenborg (1987, 2010). For a Swedenborgian argument that anxiety is not us but from outside see https://www.youtube.com/watch?v=rm9yRAx_qvU&index=14&list=PL46F098AAD5F0EA6A. Accessed on January 13, 2017.

5. Freud (2008).

6. Elster (1986, 1999).

7. Protected intimacy is a term coined by Gaston Bachelard in his book *Poetics of Space* (1969), which I developed in my book *Private Dwelling* (2004) as the particular condition that private dwelling offers.

ON LIVING TOGETHER

Perhaps the most significant achievement most of us ever attain is the one that we also take most for granted. We can do so because most others have achieved this too and, in any case, we are all merely doing what we expect to do and what is expected of us. We can take it for granted because, once we have achieved it, it is enduring and presumed always to be there. Seemingly everybody does this and it just continues on. It is accordingly something that we might notice only when we lack it or when it fails to work in the manner we have come to expect. But once we have it, and when it works well, it becomes a part of us and we are a part of it, and so we fail to see it for what it is. Yet it is so necessary and so affirming of what we are and where we are.

This great achievement is simply that we live with others. By this I do not simply mean that we are social animals. I am not referring to a community or society, a nation or a tribe. What I mean is that we live with a specific other or others: we share ourselves with a very few others and they share themselves with us. What I am concerned with then is not human sociability or even relationships as such, but a specific relationship with a very small and specific number of others and the wonderful achievement that we are able to attain and maintain such a thing; that we, in all our complexity, self-consciousness, selfishness and contrariness, are able to touch and be touched by a particular other, such that we form a permanent and lasting connection with them.

This chapter focuses on these specific relationships. It is based on a series of assumptions; or rather things that I am certain of. These are five statements that I would suggest hold in general and are necessary for us to understand how we are able to live together and retain our privacy and sense of self.

First, we live for long periods of time with the same people. Even if we are now living on our own, we will have lived with people in the past, such as our parents and siblings, and we may well live with others in the future. Living with others, and doing so for extended periods is a rather common activity.

Second, we live for long periods of time in the same place. There are certainly those who are currently transient, and there are some communities who travel (but are they then not taking their place with them?), but for most of us, most of the time, we are settled in a permanent place, and for many who are not it is something they are striving to achieve.

Third, it follows that both these people and these places matter to us very much. They are consequential to us and we become dependent on them for our well-being. Even those people and places that are now lost to us remain important to us.

Fourth, it is also clear that most of us live like this at the same time, but we do so apart. Living together in one place is a common activity. But we use these people and places to separate ourselves from other people and places that we have no connection with. We use the boundaries of place to exclude others and our connections with people face us inwards towards them and away from others.

The fifth point is that in order to understand why these people and places matter to us we have to experience them as they actually are. This means we have to see them, so to speak, when they are not being observed by those with no connection to these people or that place. Accordingly, this suggests that we have no alternative but to rely on lived experience and anecdote as our means to understand them.

When our relationships work, and also *because* they do work, we need not reflect on them: we can just live within them. We need not reflect on the minutiae of our relations and indeed to do is to stop living them. These relationships are grooved and habitual, and so appear to have their own dynamic independent of any deliberate engineering. And if or where we do seek to engineer these relationships we can quite easily despoil them by introducing a motive distinct from the mutuality of our selfless caring. These are not relationships that we can or should control, and when we try to do so they lose something significant.

These are deeply subjective relations that I wish to reflect on here, and so I wish to proceed in a subjective manner that is based on intuition, introspection and, where appropriate, anecdote. I want to look at living together in a manner that is appropriate to the nature of this relation. This means that I make no attempt to be scientific. These relations are extremely common, but they are each unique and distinct because they are personal and based on a subjective connection that cannot be predetermined. As a result the most — and perhaps only — appropriate source for such study is our own thoughts and lived experience. If it really is the case, which I believe it is, that the relations which each of us have are personal and unique to us, then we cannot generalise, or at least not beyond the simple fact that what we do is common to almost all of us.

My starting point, and also the frame into which all this fits, is precisely that place from which we start from every day. It is that thing that makes our relationships possible, and which also allows us to take them for granted. This place is our private dwelling.[1] This is the place that we share with those others who are so significant to us. It is where we are able to care and nurture, to show our love and to protect the other.[2] We can do this because of the particular facility of private dwelling that allows us to exclude unwanted others and so focus on including these particular special ones. We live within the boundary provided by private dwelling and so we are able to share in the comfort of a protected intimacy.[3] We share the space with another freely, because of the boundary that protects us, and because of that we can share of ourselves. Knowing we have this place means we can go out into the world with some sense of security, aware that there is a place and another person to whom we can return. The place, our private dwelling, frames us, maintains us and offers a beacon to guide us.

Yet private dwelling does not make us: we make it. We ourselves shape it with our lives, with our very attempts to include and exclude. It is formed out of our actions, our use of the place, as well as our memories. And all these things we can share with another. So we make the continued possibility for our own sharing out of our togetherness. We spin it ourselves: it is *homespun*.

II

I want to suggest, and to articulate in a rather straightforward, blunt and perhaps even unsophisticated way, that our experiences and our memories of things are quite literally homespun. They are created out of the fabric of our everyday domestic experience. Our experiences and memories come out of home, from our ordinary sense of self within our familiar place, and this allows us to appreciate and understand our wider place in the world as contiguous. This is because, even when our memories are made outside, they are completed, as it were, at home. They connect us like a web or a network. It is this sense of being in place that provides us with the complacency[4] to spin out the significance of these external experiences and memories as meaningful entities.

The idea of being homespun has a particular meaning. We should note immediately that to call someone or something 'homespun' is not to praise or compliment them. The word is usually taken to refer to an argument, philosophy or an idea that is plain or unsophisticated. It is indeed straightforward and blunt with no attempt at finesse. That which is homespun can often be seen to be artless and coarse. It might be perceived as inelegant, plain and without a clear sense that it is finished. It might still appear to be rough and rustic. To be homespun is to be unpolished and, of course, it is to be homemade. There is no glamour here, nothing sophisticated, but merely the crude and unvarnished attempt to create something from what is around us. There is a suggestion here of a lack of guile, of no cunning, that 'what you see is what you get'. There is just surface and no depth, with little that is worthy of investigation or further study.

Of course we need not see homespun in this way, or only in this manner. There is, we might suggest, some virtue in being straightforward, of being without any side or cunning, and of being open and honest, and so for us presenting things as they really do seem to be. There is nothing behind or beyond what we say and what we have to offer. There is no duplicity here, no attempt to connive and no ulterior motive. And this is because what we see is precisely what we think we should get.

We should also remind ourselves that what is homemade is always bespoke. It is not mass produced, but made to order and for a particular purpose. It is not produced on an industrial scale out of standardised parts, but made to fit the needs of a particular person at a particular time. The homespun operates on a level that is close to us and which we can understand. It has a particularity in that it relates to just ourselves within those circumstances in which we find ourselves.

For a thing to be homespun it is created from home — homemade — and so it does not come from any external source. It is not factory-made and nor will we necessarily find it in any library or seminar room. The homespun does not derive from any investigations out there in the world, but instead derives out of us — and only us — being at home. The homespun is a reflection from where we feel we belong based on what we know and have around us. We make a universe for ourselves, a world of meaning and significance, by our home-based spinning. We create our world not through visiting and exploring, but by returning to our own private space and, through the efficacy of this privacy, spinning our experiences into sense. This does not mean that we should never go out or that we should not investigate and explore other places. What it does mean though is that we are only able to make sense of these things external to us because of our capability to dwell privately and because of the nature of our existence as private households where we live with particular others. We can understand them because we can bring them home and connect them with what we already know and use. So we spin the significance of our lives out of our experiences, whilst being within a sheltered place, within the confines of sense we call private dwelling.[5]

This sense of the homespun allows us to adopt and adapt the outside world to our private dwelling and to do so in a manner that places no constraints on our complacency. We need to ensure we are not challenged or that our sense of our place in the world is being subverted. Instead we absorb new experiences and operationalise their meaning through their integration into our private dwelling. They add to an already existing network of experiences and memories. This network is spun at home, within the fastness of private dwelling, out of the relationships made within the dwelling, the intimacies formed and strengthened there, and which we then take out into the world as a template for meaningfulness. This network or web is what helps us to catch new experiences that we can then in time add to our collection.

So we should properly see the homespun as a framework and as a process. It is what we live within, but it also what we continually engage with in order to create and maintain our world. Its purpose is to hold us, but also to help us filter out some of the complexity of our world. Accordingly, it is quite right to see the homespun as a process of simplification, of ordering and the creation of a commonality of view. The homespun view does not ignore the complexity of things, and nor does it forget how the world really is in all its diversity and difference. But it does modify the world to make it fit into our place. It helps us to know the world and for us to see that the world can appear as there for us. We might see this as a necessary illusion that allows us to become and remain settled.

But illusion or not, is there not perhaps a danger that this whole idea of the homespun being seen as sentimental? Indeed, some might argue that the whole idea of writing subjectively about living with others can all too easily slip into excessive sentiment. While there is undoubtedly a danger of this, we have to recognise that there is a real distinction between sentiment and sentimentality, between the heartfelt connection with something or someone and its idealisation. Sentiment relates to our feeling, to our closeness and our associations with others. It might be where we place emotion over reason. But the test here is whether we allow the emotion to control us. Sentiment, we might suggest, is based on necessary but moderated emotion, but where it becomes excessive we slip into sentimentality, which is an exaggerated or indulgent form of emotion.

Sentimentality is frequently eschewed because it is considered to be both tasteless and unrealistic. On the one hand, it can be seen as mawkish and softheaded, lacking any real substance. On the other hand, it can be seen as divorced from reality, and lacking a proper sense of proportion. It is simply lacking in reason and consequently can be seen as extreme and disproportionate. When something is sentimental there is often just too much of it.

But do we not want and expect our relations with our loved ones to be based on emotion rather than reason? We are not with these particular people because of some rational calculation or cost-benefit analysis. There has to be some tenderness that the relationship is founded on that transcends calculation. Our relations generate sentiment and emotion precisely because they are based on something significant.

So it is not really a matter of emotion *or* reason, but rather a matter of balance between the two. We keep our emotions, and therefore excessive sentiment, in bounds by reason, and in particular by the recognition of our place alongside this other person in our shared space. The closeness of the relationship may be because of tenderness, intimacy and, of course, emotion. But we still retain a sense of the otherness of the person we are with and that we are distinct from others even as they are ours and we are theirs.

We also have to recognise that the judging of excess, of what is deemed to be sentimental, is itself subjective: sentimentality, as it were, is in the eye of the beholder. What might be seen as proportionate within a relationship might seem excessive from the outside. Actions and emotions may appear indulgent to those not part of the relationship. But then these actions and emotions are not meant for them and for them to view them is either a violation or an accident. Our relations with others are simply not meant to be seen from the outside. So if sentimentality within subjective relations is judged externally, we should be suspicious of it and precisely because it is external.

A discussion on the specificity of togetherness will always risk the accusation of sentimentality. We are dealing here with the emotionality, the uniqueness and the absolute irreplaceability of the other all within a place that is special to each of them. The stakes here are really quite high, in that we are concerned with what is quite fundamental to our individuality, namely, the specificity of our relationship with another and its meaning to both of us. The challenge then is to capture this closeness and uniqueness without any excess of sentiment.

A point allied to the accusation of sentimentality is to suggest that a discussion of the homespun, conducted through introspection and anecdote, is not really a legitimate topic for academic discourse. It might be said that this is not, properly speaking, an *intellectual* discussion. It is too trite and inconsequential in the face of the great issues and concerns of the day. Moreover, the introspective method eschews theory and any sense of a grand narrative and so gives us too little from which to make general statements. But again, why should we fall into this trap when discussing the subjective within its own context? We are not seeking to get beyond the subjective, but instead to experience it from close to. We are seeking to recognise and respect the very specificity of subjective experience rather than trying to compose some form of abstract general subjectivism.

We are seeking to explore the specificity of our subjective relations and to do so in a manner that allows us to say something significant. However, we have to appreciate that we cannot become too general and abstract out of this subjectivity. Indeed, we should perhaps see abstraction as worse than sentimentality. That which is homespun is never abstract, but a concrete form made from what we find just there around us. If this places some limits on what we are considering and on what conclusions we seek to make, then it should be considered a price worth paying.

III

We often see our lives in two distinct ways. On one level, which we could perhaps call the *continuous present*, we live in what appears to us as a continuum. Our life seems to be a relatively seamless, continuous and contiguous existence, in which one second runs into the next. We can see this as a continuous *now*: of our current, but continuing existence, as a being in the world. But on another level, which we can call the *impressionistic*, we see our lives as a series of discrete events or impressions, of singular events which all appear to us as separate and qualitatively distinct from each other.

The difference between these two levels is essentially between the present and the past, between action and memory. But the distinction can also be seen in a different way that has implications for our senses of dwelling and of place more generally. The idea of *now* relates directly with the external, with the connection with the world, and the notion that the objective is also always social. But the level of discrete impressions is internal, and consists of those things that register, or rather now *only* register, to us as being meaningful and significant as past events. These things have come from out of the world: they are, as it were, past *nows*. Accordingly, they register to us now only as memories, and as meaningful by being absorbed into us and taking on a particular register as singularities within our own consciousness.

What connects the two conceptions of *now* is the particular manner of their creation, or rather the very process of how we absorb things into ourselves, whereby apparently objective actions in the world — what we might term the continuous stream of current acts — becomes segmented and parts of it are then given a singular resonance as memories, as impressions of events and things, and so, in their way, they become events in themselves, as representations of other events, just as a photograph of an object is distinct from that object.

We can see that these two levels — the continuous present and the impressionistic — are connected and depend on each other, even as we insist as seeing them as separate. So, for example, the internal impressionistic sense impacts on the continuous present, by focussing us onto certain elements of a place, action or event, and it is these snippets of memory that determine how we act in the present in terms of how we now deal with that place and how we relate to those who are there with us. If we now consider a particular place or person, we become rather more directed, or perhaps we could say circumscribed, by the impressions we already have of that person or place. This might manifest itself as a refusal to see that person or to return to that place. This, in the circumstances we are in, in this time we define as *now*, may be entirely unfair and based on a less than balanced view. But that — unbalanced — is precisely what impressions are. Our impressions may lead us to an unfounded perception of a person or of a place.

Yet we might always be prepared to persuade ourselves that our impressions, which we should remember are always singular, subjective and non-divisible — they are ours, having been generated by us — are also incapable of being 'wrong' or unfounded. Indeed what would it mean to say that our impressions are 'wrong'? Perhaps we should admit that the word 'wrong' is not the most appropriate or even correct term for the process. Impressions form unconsciously and are non-intentional and non-deliberative. Therefore they cannot be wrong, as such. What we have to avoid here is the language and processes of an objective rationality and instead rely on rather more inchoate processes that are not delimited by formal procedures. There is no logic or rationality in the formation of our impressions. We can point to reasons for our associations, but these are just personal and reasonable only to us. The processes involved in the formation of impressions are almost entirely contingent, in that we have no choice but to start from where we currently are and with the circumstances that pertain now. Hence the impressionistic depends on the continuous present: our impressions are literally what we find at our feet.

But this contingency limits the level of control that we have. We might see the world as a network or a web, where all is in touch with everything else, and where nothing is independent of something else. At certain times, we might convince ourselves that we are at the centre of this web, with things contacting us and emanating out from us. We take ourselves as the very centre and act accordingly. We, after all, are the ones doing the spinning. But there is, properly speaking, no centre in a continuous web. There is no objective central point around which everything else revolves or resolves itself. We are all, despite whatever illusions we might have, at the periphery. Our 'centre' is merely an insignificant part of an amorphous and seemingly unlimited expanse of connections. What we are spinning might be connected to a whole, but this is not something that we can control and which we are able to manage. We are not even able to see it all. It is for this very reason that we will point to the impressionistic and insist that this really is our world, for it is only at this level that we can believe that we create and so hope for any sense of controlling what is around us. What makes being in a connected world manageable, or even liveable, is that we focus on what is close to us, and that what we focus on becomes even closer to us as a result. What is important is so because it is close to, and it is close to us because it is important. Only part of the world can ever be like this to us. We cannot hold everything close to us and we cannot focus on all of it. We cannot understand the entire world, and so we focus on only a fraction of it.

Precisely how much of the world we can focus on is not prescribed or predetermined, and how much we know of the world is an open issue and cannot be foretold and cannot be presumed. However, what we know of the world derives from those parts of it that are close, from those parts of it that do touch us. We know of the world because of our connections with it. All the actions that we take are themselves world disclosing, creating impressions out of the continuous present. As we proceed we open up the world. But we proceed as part of the world, developing and changing it, like a ripple in a pool. And like a ripple in a pool, we are not distinct from the world. We stand out for a time, perhaps casting impressions onto others as we do, before being subsumed again into the whole.

We live in what we take to be now, but we spin our home, our sense of where are and who we are, from what impressions we have gleaned and taken out from this continuous present. This means that we see ourselves as distinct, as the centre of our own network. We need this illusion, and we need to convince ourselves that it is not an illusion, and once we are able to do this we are able to spin ourselves out towards those very few others that attract us.

IV

Being in place can mean being with another. It is where we share with some people, but only some people, with those who we have chosen to be with. We have found a solid place where we can be alone with others, and this sharing does not diminish our experience of the place. We do not feel crowded or harassed by the presence of others. Instead the being together enhances and magnifies this place for us. It enhances the significance of the place and seems to deepen the bond we have for it. Being able to share what is *mine* with others, so that we refer to it as *ours*, makes it a bigger place.

Living together contains much of what we are. It is being close to at least one other person. There is a tenderness that comes with that closeness. We change the other by our closeness, by proximity, by attention, by love and by care, and they can change us with the same equipment. This is something that can endure. Time does not circumscribe the wonder of togetherness. Togetherness does not get tired.

But there is also a matter-of-factness and a complacency that derives out of togetherness. There need be no fuss or show over someone who is always here. It need not be demonstrative. Living together is the closeness to know when a little distance is needed. We might see it as the absence of absence, where we are still present even when we are not physically here: we can be and we will be, and so we are still here.

So we might say that being together is a mix of the taken-for-grantedness of shared activities and experiences, and the sublime quality of being allowed to be with the most special person who, we feel, has ever lived. We combine everyday sharing without fuss or show of emotion with an irreplaceable closeness.

Living together is the sublime distinctiveness of the absolutely familiar. It is that look; that smile; that gesture; those things that only we seem to notice and this is because only we are let in. Living together is simply the other being there as we know them to be. We can speculate on this familiarity: do we love someone because they are familiar, or are they now so familiar because of the love we have for them? Did we grow to love this someone so deeply because of proximity, or is the proximity a result of an initial attraction? But whatever the case, we quickly realise that being together is not just a matter of proximity, but of *licit proximity*. It is a closeness that has no need for excuses and further explanation. What matters is that we are allowed and expected to be this close.

Within this licit proximity there is trust. We feel strongly that our feelings are reciprocated and there is a mutuality. But we can ever be sure of this mutuality. Does the other feel the same as we do? Is there a real fusing together here? Does the other truly reciprocate? Of course, we can never truly know. The only means we have is the very closeness we experience with that person. All we can do is trust what the other tells us. And they, of course, have no option but to trust us and what we tell them. Just as we cannot know what the other really thinks, how can the other really know precisely how we feel. There is no unmediated way we can elicit what each other really is thinking and what they truly mean other than by trusting them. It would almost certainly be the case that our feelings for each other would not be sustainable if they were not reciprocated in a near similar fashion. We could not maintain proximity without some reciprocity for long without it starting to harm us. So togetherness means trust and this can only be demonstrated over time: to be trusted, then, is to be reliable and to repay the trust shown in us. In other words, we remain trusted so long as we do not betray that trust.

But this trust is often not demonstrative in that it is folded into togetherness and is not in any way observable as a separate entity. The trust we have for another is shown in our continued proximity. Like us, the other demonstrates their trust through care and by always being there. We never feel we are separate, never consider that we are apart. This is a very particular form of proximity that need not be physical, but is rather based on commitment and a sense of permanence. It continues precisely because we take it be enduring.

Living together is where we do not share with the many in order that we can share with this one other. Our lives are only possible because we have learned the importance of relative distance. We have learned how far we must keep from some and how close we must be to others, when to move closer and when to shift away. This is not a science but an art that involves our judgement to discern how close we should be to others for our comfort and theirs. It is only through the recognition of boundaries that we can share. It is only because of our ability to exclude that we can include. And to include we must enclose some and exclude others. Our togetherness demands our separation from others. We have to discriminate, and we have to hope that most others remain indifferent to us. Without exclusion no one could really be *here*. This place is made by deliberate exclusion — a locked door and closed curtains — and by the self-exclusion of others who are too busy to notice what we do. We depend on the voluntary exile of those we will never meet and will never know. We rely on the indifference of others just as we happily, benignly, necessarily, ignore them. We do not know where they are. We only know that they are not *here*. If it were ever to occur to us, we might thank them for their indifference and, in return, expect gratitude for our unawareness of them. In the meantime, their indifference will do.

Togetherness works by reducing interference, by enclosing us and excluding unwanted others. We are able to focus our gaze inwards and limit our contact with those on the outside to the level that we can manage. We know that there is an outside and that it is populated by people just like us. We have no fear of them and wish them no harm, but they are where we wish them to be. We want them to stay on the outside, apart from us.

The strength of sharing is such that others cannot penetrate. They can only sit on the outside waiting to be admitted. But they can only gain access when it is freely given. It cannot be forced; there can be little conscious effort. Where it is forced it ceases to be any real form of togetherness, and so anyone outside must wait for acceptance. If and when this acceptance comes we seldom recognise its significance. To accept someone means to take them as they are such that we need not think of them as anything other than ours: the acceptance would not be mutual if we could see it. And so it now appears to us that being part of the sharing is where we have always been. The relationship has no start and can have no end. In sharing there is no before or after and it is not conditional. Sharing comes with little or no reflection on the consequences of what we are doing: we are too busy being inside.

Accordingly, there is very little show. Tenderness is often manifested by matter-of-factness not by extravagant shows of affection. Living together is straightforward, no nonsense, habitual, grooved and informal. Its strength shows in the liberties we can take and the corners we can cut, and also in knowing where the limits to the corner cutting and liberties are. The continuity of togetherness comes from a knowledge of others and a preparedness to let the other know. There is no longer a need for any performance. We need only to be there so we can be theirs. All we need to be close is stability. We need to be at the same pace, to be in time when we move.

So togetherness is both a tie and a boundary: it keeps us close while ensuring that others are a way off. Togetherness encloses us; it wraps us up. But we can still move, together and separately. However, we can move in our space and in our time, alongside another who shares the very same freedoms.

Being with another is to have another pole. One is attracted to that pole and it provides something beyond us to focus on. It forces us to move beyond our selfish concerns as we are pulled into their orbit. The person we love, who we are in step with, remains a separate individual. They do not become a part of us. We cannot control them; we are not them and they are not us. Yet we are prepared to sacrifice much of what we have and are for them. We feel that we cannot be anywhere else but with them. We do this precisely because they are an individual and so distinct from us. Vladmir Solovyov, in his book *The Meaning of Love*,[6] tells us that 'The meaning of human love, speaking generally, is the justification and salvation of individuality through the sacrifice of egoism'.[7] It is only by giving up our internal boundaries, which we might otherwise use to promote ourselves above all others, and so come together with another, that we truly find our individuality. In a sense, we complete ourselves by giving up on our self-interest and joining with another. We can do this, Solovyov argues, because the meaning of love is to recognise the absolute significance of another, who, in turn, sees that absolute significance in us. But, for each of us, it remains an absolute.

Togetherness does not subsume individuality. Our individuality fits within togetherness and combines with another. Living together is a mutuality, a oneness. But 'mine' and 'me' still remain and are enhanced by the sharing. The word 'ours' makes 'mine' expand: we are not diminished by the sharing. We become more than simply 'mine + mine'. It is not a simple aggregation. We become a larger *one* that is itself distinct from 'mine' and 'mine' while also enclosing them both. We are greater than just two people. 'Ours' means that there is a greater 'mine' for each of us. Indeed, it might be better to suggest that, strictly speaking, we do not share 'ours'. Each of us has it exclusively. It can only exist where it is whole and each of us has all of it.

Being one together is greater than two apart. Each of us has more and is greater than on our own, and this applies even when we spend a lot of time being apart from the people we live with. We are apart while at work, or while doing separate activities. We may be apart for days or weeks, and perhaps even longer. But we still are together and we know that we are. The commitment is still there, the same connection remains. We know the other cares for us and we care for them; we matter to them and so we can deal with a temporary separation. We do not feel that we are truly apart because the relationship goes on. The dwelling is still full of the other's presence: their clothes, their books, their smell. They are still there because it is still their home where they belong. It is still theirs, mine and ours.

But how close do we ever truly get to another person? They remain a separate person, with their own thoughts and feelings. We can influence another's thoughts and feeling, and they can affect ours. Most assuredly, by our actions we can absolutely ruin the lives by another, and we can, of course, enhance their lives considerably by our care and kindness. But the other remains distinct, even as we share all we have with them.

Accordingly, there may well be fighting and competition in a relationship, but also a recognition of the stakes in play. We are often most angered by those closest to us. It matters much more what they say and do: they say and do it *for* you and *to* you. The test of any relationship is its consequentiality: that we know it matters and that it always has done. And so we might not seek to over-test the elasticity of what binds us. There is a duty in our togetherness such that there is no distinction between giving and taking. It is in not having to think twice about giving and never for a moment seeing it as a sacrifice. It is growing through giving. Both bring the same joy to us. Indeed there may be sorrow in not sharing: in not having to, not wanting to, and in not being able to.

What wouldn't we give for the other? Would we really sacrifice ourselves? Would we really do anything? We might see this as the true test, even if we are actually reluctant to really find out. We often say we would do sacrifice ourselves for the other: 'I would do anything for you?' But would we really go so far? Are there actually limits to what we would do and act? Most of the time, for most of us, these limits are never tested, and so we do not really know what lengths we would go to protect our loved ones. We like to think that we know, and that we are convinced that we would go to any length to protect them. But how do we know we really would? We certainly hope never to have to find out. We will pledge our unconditionality and we hear the same back, and this undoubtedly gives us some comfort. But we can also be reasonably sure that there will be no occasion when we have to face such a trial. We know that others have faced this situation, and we can empathise and appreciate the horror of the situation. But we are grateful that we have been spared this. What we wish to do, within the comfort granted by our pledges of unconditionality, is to live an ordinary life together.

In any case, both parties in a relationship might not feel the same. One may have deeper or stronger feelings than the other. One may feel that this is a match for life while the other sees it just as a pleasant but brief fling. Motives and aims differ, and why shouldn't they? Why should two people, even those attracted to each other, think alike? This does not invalidate the comments about the shared significance of a relationship. But this suggests that we should not idealise our, or any other, relationship.

In a certain manner we all still live alone. This is because others can only get so close. Another cannot share our head-space. They cannot feel as we feel and know as we know. They can only get as close as we let them. So, in part, we are always alone, within the solid boundary of our skull and within the limits of our ability to communicate with another. With another we are never without the need for mediation, for interpretation, and this can create misunderstanding and resentment. But it is the art of togetherness that allows us to forget this, to minimise any distance and to act as if we are one. We teach ourselves, through closeness, to forget the distance between my head and yours.

We act together, but this is not always the same as acting as one. We can seek to minimise our individuality, but we can only do this ourselves, as a separate individual, by consciously transferring from 'mine' to 'ours'. At best we can share with another. But we should remember the purpose of this is precisely due to their being another who wishes to share with us, to subsume part of them into a greater 'us'. It is the very separateness of the other, and that therefore they can be close to us, that matters to us. It really is significant that they are not us, that they are a different and distinct person. It is that we can lean on them and them on us, that we support each other and that we are close to them, but not them.

So the idea of 'being with' can never be extinguished. We are, so to speak, only together 'as one' in so far as we are two, only because there is a separate other who is prepared, just as you are, to minimise the separatedness between us. But there will always be some distance and it is proper to say that it is in that very distance that togetherness can be found. Togetherness is found in the distance between us. There is a true equality and evenness in this distance.

We might see living together as a life sentence where we have committed ourselves. And we are most certainly committed when we are there: we always go in as if it is for life. It starts with an optimism and a hope for something special, and this is not diminished by the routines which we develop together. But we do not stay at this exalted level, and this is because of the very routines we have to establish.

When we wish to be with someone we seek to include them into what we take as important and meaningful. We wish to show them things, share our experiences, to make them part of these things. We validate our experiences in the light of our togetherness, and our togetherness can, in turn, be validated by the experience of sharing of something that is so important to us.

In living together we accept another, for what they are and what they have. We change by choice, or rather by a giving way that is often not recognised as such. We are not aware of our amendments and focus instead on the other and our closeness to them. The choice is in the initial commitment and we do not necessarily keep a tally, or even remain aware, of the concessions we have made. Our actions are akin to the effects of the tide on a pebble. The tide changes the pebble by a slow, inexorable, gentle and regular force. It slowly rounds off any rough edges and creates a smooth and even surface. The effect is due to regularity and consistency rather than through being harsh and abrasive. We do not rub or grate but caress. There is an implacability in this, but we seldom notice it in the gentle wash of our togetherness.

There is indeed something in this image of gentle change. We might suggest that togetherness drifts rather than moves in any positive manner. A relationship has no direction and no purpose other than its own continuance. To change the metaphor, it is like a bubble drifting on a breeze.

Togetherness has no outside. It is only truly apparent from the inside. From the outside there are just two people, and we might easily only notice one of them: an attractive man or woman. Or it might be that we only know one of the parties in a relationship. The other person is less known to us, and so we do not see them equally.

But in any case, we see them on our terms and not theirs, from our perspective and what interests us, what catches our eye. We know that many others are together, but we cannot know what it means for them except in the most general of terms. Indeed, how could we ever know more than that? We are not party to this relationship. We may know that there is a relationship here, but we can only view it through our own experience.

It might appear that having a child or finding a partner is so arbitrary. A child is the combination of one of hundreds of eggs released over a 30- to 40-year period and one of tens of millions of sperm. But once they are together and the child is created, there is no longer anything in the least arbitrary about it. We give that new person a name and they become their name and no other one could now possibly fit. Whilst any name might have been possible, and deemed suitable, before birth, once named it is fixed and so obviously appropriate as to be absurd now to consider anything else. In hindsight, giving a child this name seems inevitable. More significantly perhaps, our responsibility as a parent becomes absolute and permanent. We cannot put away this responsibility and act as if the child had never been born.

There is also something arbitrary about when two people are attracted to each other. All previous relationships, entered into by these two people with optimism and hope, have not worked out. Perhaps this might have been due to the feelings and actions of only one party and the other might have wished the relationship to continue. In other circumstances this past relationship would still be a fact. Or it might be that the meeting between these two people comes about by accident or chance. The merest of changes in years, weeks or even minutes before could have so altered the path of their life that it would have prevented them from coming together. They may never have even met, had never been available, or even have been looking for anyone. Of course, we should not presume that there is only person who could make us happy, that only person out of six billion would have done for us. In other times, and in other circumstances, someone else might have been even more special or at least just as good for us. Yet this did not happen and cannot now happen. Once we are in a relationship it seems to have been inevitable, preordained even, and the only thing that will change this is if, for whatever reason, the relationship ends.

The fact that we are not looking any longer is important and essential to togetherness. Of course, we notice others and may well find plenty of people attractive and engaging. We do not ignore others or fail to notice what qualities they may have. But, having found a partner, we now tend to focus inwards towards the specific other and no longer outwards. We see those outside in a different manner now, as if we only see them through the frame provided by the other. Being together with this one we are complacent, settled and without focus for others. This might be little more than inertia, where the comfortableness of the relationship keeps us together. But, more positively, it is the togetherness, the passion of and for each other, such that we know each other so well and that in a way no one else ever can, that leave us with the feeling that we can now, and in the future, have no other.

There is clearly more to a relationship that the initial reaction. We need more than this. We may see someone who is good to look at and find them interesting and engaging company. But this might not be enough. What we have to find is some unique quality in that other person, some distinctiveness. And importantly, we have to find that sense of distinctiveness is being reciprocated. There will be a sexual desire, but there must also be an especially focused tenderness that is not exhausted by this desire. This tenderness is not generalised but instead is focused onto a very specific being, and this is because of who that being is.

When we are out in the world we are often still with those we are close to. They are either literally with us or we still feel they are close to us. This sense of closeness offers us a carapace, some protection from the world, from its indifference, its busyness and its all too apparent ignorance of us. We have the love of and for another to protect us. This, we might say, is a background comfort. It is always there, but infrequently called upon, like carrying a lucky pebble in one's pocket. We know it's there and find comfort in this, even though most of the time we do not call upon it. But we can call upon it to help us if we feel we need it. So we do not, so to speak, go out unprotected. We have a token, a talisman, to protect us. We do not have to use it for its significance to remain apparent.

This is what carries us, although it is mostly not thought about and not at the front of our mind. The other is always present, always there. They will be there for us. It really does not need thought. It transcends thinking, being the 'is-ness' of our existential completeness. Our sense of the other is a peculiar form of taken-for-grantedness, in that they are the most special, irreplaceable, priceless and incomparable person to us. Yet, they are absolutely dependable and always there. This is undoubtedly a heady mix and not without its emotional ups and downs. Yet when we are together there is a sense of completeness, of comfort and of care. We are being cared for by the most special person. But, we both know too that we live with a flawed person, a person who is special to not many besides ourselves. There is nothing really particular about them, apart from the fact that they are mine and we are theirs. Any relationship will have its problems. There will be arguments, misunderstandings and conflicts. It may eventually end. But while it lasts, it will contain an unconditionality and closeness that cannot be replicated, and to which nothing — literally nothing — can compare.

V

We had a life before we met our special other and we bring this with us into our relationship. There are people we know, places that are important to us, ideas, views, arguments and memories that we all carry with us wherever we go and, because they are so significant to us, we wish to share them with this special one. But in doing so we change these people, places and memories. The other changes how they look, how they act and what they mean to us. They can be validated, which is what we would hope for, or they can be diminished, and so there is a risk involved in the sharing.

I had not been back to Bradford, the place where I was a student, for over 12 years. But the atmosphere of the place felt the same. Or rather it was nearly the same. I had spent four years there as an undergraduate and had visited often over the five years I studied part-time for my doctorate. What was different now was that I was with my wife and daughters: I was showing this important place to my family, and this, I must admit, worried me.

I had the same sense of anticipation as I always had when getting near to the city; a feeling of opportunity and freedom. This feeling did not exactly derive from when I was an undergraduate there, but from a decade later and the infrequent visits, perhaps only two or three times a year, I would make when I was doing my PhD. This feeling was one of returning, of coming back to a place that was formative. But it was also a feeling of an intellectual opening up, of moving in a direction I wanted to go, that gaining a PhD would open up a new life for me as an academic rather than a public sector worker. Bradford, I felt, was the one place where I had been free to be myself for the first time, being away from parents and having to become self-reliant. So returning a decade later as a part-time postgraduate student was like regaining this freedom, if only for a day, and being able to forget finances, mortgages, meetings in my diary and so on. I could put aside all those 'grown-up' things associated with working for a living. There was undoubtedly a contradiction here: of combining an initial sense of self-reliance with a later sense of freedom from responsibility.

So when the train got past New Pudsey station and reached the outskirts of Bradford, with the first sight of Manningham Mill on one side and then, when a bit nearer, the University's Richmond building on the other, I felt I was back and had that surge of well-being and excitement that I used to get in the late 1980s and early 1990s when coming up for supervision meetings. But this time I was able to try to explain the feeling to B, H and R. I had seen B's eagerness when we went through Newcastle where she had studied; she would look out of the train window, picking out the landmarks; the bridges, the Baltic Exchange, looking at what had altered and was new — the Angel of the North on the way in, the Millennium Bridge, the rebuilt St James Park and the Sage Music Centre looking like a slug wrapped in tin foil sitting on the banks of the Tyne. So B knew how I felt, even if she laughed at the unexpected enthusiasm and gaucheness of my telling.

My old university was having what it called 'the Big Reunion' to celebrate its 40th birthday. This is perhaps not much of a history, but it contained a hefty proportion of mine, and that was why it was important for me to join in. But I did not arrange to meet anybody up there, and nor did

I check on the lists available to see who had said they were coming. And I met no one I knew. I saw a few faces I thought I recognised, but no one to speak to, and perversely, this was exactly what I wanted. What I was keen to do was to meet the place and not the people who were there with me at the time. I wanted to see what was still there and what had altered, to see how much of it I could still call *mine* 28 years since I first arrived there and 12 years since my last visit when I struggled with a PhD gown the colour of tomato soup on a very hot July day.

I found on the campus that much had altered, with new buildings where there had been waste ground and car parks. The Richmond Building, a 10 storey stone-clad building built in the mid-1960s was undergoing a face-lift and was being covered in a very fashionable light blue cladding. We went in the lift up to the top of the building and I remembered the sense of vertigo I would get looking down the stairway from N floor. H and R dared each other to look down and then kept doing it. The view from the window at the top of the building was magnificent, with a panorama of Bradford and a distant view of the hills.

Going down to the main foyer of the building we got to see an example of what I loved about the place, its almost sublime eccentricity, a strangeness that seems to be entirely natural there and so is taken for granted by everyone. We looked out of one of the plate glass windows on the ground floor at the back of the main foyer. There on the wide stone windowsill was the nest of a mistle thrush. The bird sat there stock-still and we thought it might be a model, put there as a student prank or part of some art installation. But eventually the mistle thrush moved and we caught site of the beaks of the little chicks below her. As we looked a couple of the catering staff stopped by and told us, in their matter of fact way, that they had watched her building the nest and sit on the eggs. The nest had become part of the background of their daily lives as they worked in the café in the foyer. They talked about the bird as if she had always been there and that it could not be more natural for a mistle thrush to perch up against plate glass on a stone window ledge in full view of thousands of students passing by each day.

'But there's heatin' vent just below her, love.' One of the caterers said, and the other nodded. And so we moved off back to the centre of the day's attractions, and I remembered why I loved this place, and any worries I had dissipated.

What mattered to me that day, and why I was a bit worried, was how B, H and R would react to the place, and whether they would share my feelings for the city and the University. I was concerned that they would find the day boring or dislike Bradford. B was no fan of the city, having visited a few times. She claimed it had always been bleak and dull, and my idle speculations about one day getting a job up there were always met with a firm 'No!'

But they loved the day, the fun of running up and down the tiers of the grassed terrace by the Library, now rather grandly referred to as the 'Amphitheatre'. We watched a succession of students putting on padded sumo suits to barge into each other and clown around. The girls could not contain their laughter, even on the tenth occasion of watching a pair of drunken students hurl themselves at each other. B and I had a genuine Bradford curry, my first in over 20 years, as we sat on picnic benches at the top of the terrace and listened to an old ska band playing on the stage below us.

The importance of this visit was that it was a major place, a formative place for me, but, and this is the main point, one prior to meeting B and the birth of both H and R. This was one place, so important to me, where they did not, and could not, have figured. So it mattered for me to try to share it with them, to bring this earlier and hugely significant part of my life to them as an offering. I felt it was part indulgence: 'Look, this is me, what formed me, what made me. Do you like it?' But it was also a sharing, a giving *of me*, a telling tales about myself, and with this came a reticence, a little fear that they would not accept it, not understand or appreciate its importance to me, that they might not see the place as I did.

Yet what I now most remember of the day is the being together, the closeness, and the girls being themselves in this place that they were hitherto not a part of, and where the memories were exclusively my own. But they enjoyed it on their terms, they accepted the place, and it accepted them. The day then was memorable, a validation of that part of my life; and as a fun day out, which was the only level it could have worked for the girls. It was a simple informal day structured around memories I had and the importance of being together.

So we now have shared memories, and when I think of Bradford now I think of that day together and not just of those over 25 years ago. This new day had overlaid those older memories and it is still stronger, newer, more colourful, and more alive. Bradford, as a place, has been topped up, but also altered, and I think this is because it is now shared, so that this newer experience of the place over-rides, or over-writes, the earlier memories and the feeling of the place that I had built up before. I no longer see the place as I did because of them.

This is part of what I take Paul Shepheard[8] to mean when he says we should see our actions on the world as a wonderful thing. Places and things are significant to us because they manifest our presence: they are all that we have to show for our existence in this world. If we cannot celebrate this, if we are unable to see anything worthwhile in what we have, then why, we must ask, are we here? And what, apart from oblivion, is the alternative?

VI

There are times when we are alone. The issue is often not that we have no contacts at all, but rather that we are unable to be in contact with anyone at that particular moment. We are away from them and cannot connect to them as we would like. They are committed to other things and so are we. Or perhaps we have drifted apart from each other, or the other may no longer wish us to be in touch. So there are some people we know, who know us, and we may well know a lot about each other, but we cannot get in contact. Our attempts to reach out are inconvenient, unheard or unwanted. So there may be a lack or closeness, and it might be temporary or permanent.

While much of our lives derive from arbitrary actions, our relationships can seem definitive and almost pre-ordained. Once they have happened we cannot imagine an alternative path and have no desire to plot one. But we might regret an action or an omission, and wanted to have done something different to what we actually found ourselves doing. However, we might wish that we had done this not instead of the chosen path, but as well as. We wish that this could be an addition to our experiences and not instead of them. We want what we have missed but not to forego much of what we have gained or done since. So what regrets we have are safe and non-threatening; they are wistful rather than deeply consequential. We might see it as a soft regret because we do not wish to forego much of what has occurred since. We can safely dwell on these acts or omissions from within the gentle cradle of our living together with another. We can think of what might have been without putting at risk what we have. Of course, there are regrets that cannot be so easily assuaged. The scale of the loss may be too great.

There are many tiny regrets in our lives, things that spring into our minds without any apparent reason, and which give us a moment's pause. There might even be a slight cringe or sense of embarrassment. But we will soon forget and move on, perhaps wishing as we do that we were not such a shallow or flawed character and promising ourselves to do better in the future. But these regrets are now so minor that we never actually do anything to reform ourselves.

We are largely successful in hiding these thoughts away. We tend to be very good at organising our lives so that we need not reflect on our failings. We use the present to ward off the past. The very busyness of our present provides us with a refuge from the failings of our past.

But some relationships do indeed end, and there is always sadness for a relationship that can no longer grow. Indeed, once a relationship has ended, we might even think that there is also something cruel, intended or otherwise, in the indifference of a former intimate. They are no longer there, no longer close, and nor do they wish to be, despite what we may still feel about them and what we might still hope for. There is no longer that reciprocity, that togetherness, that easy informality, that casual, but so meaningful, proximity. We cannot believe that this person we were just so close to can now have the resolve to turn away from us. How can they be that cruel? After all we still love them (or we want to). How can what they now feel so outweigh what we once (thought or assumed) we had? Have we really misjudged them so badly and are they really not the person we took them to be? How can intimacy shift to indifference so quickly? We feel impotent and unable to act. There is little or nothing we can do save plead and humiliate ourselves in the face of this apparently implacable cruelty. Slowly we come to accept the ending of this relationship, and that this person will no longer be part of our life. But we still know them. We retain our memories of those shared intimacies. We remember the closeness and perhaps even the promises, all apparently sincerely meant, that we each made. These memories are now clouded, and perhaps they might become crowded out by the fixity of that implacable unsmiling face we thought we knew and by a closed door that we can no longer open.

What often hurts us the most about a failed relationship is knowing that a person who we were once so close to is now permanently distant from us, and that there is nothing we can do to change this. We might still be willing, desperate even, but they are not prepared for us to be near them. What upsets us, and creates such a longing in us, is the difference between the former closeness and the distance that exists now. There is no longer any possibility of intimacy.

We will get over this, often by getting close to someone else, and so we can come to realise that this person, who is now lost to us, was perhaps not actually really that special after all. However, some of the regret and longing may still remain, even if it is no longer painful. We focus on 'what might have been' and become wistful and, if we are fortunate, we might become able to focus on the good times we had rather than being tormented by its ending.

VII

Living together, properly speaking, is never negative, it is never abusive, and this is because negativity and abuse are not togetherness. Abuse is domination of one over the other. There is no 'ours' in this case, only a selfish dominating 'mine' that subsumes the other. It is where one person is being used by the other. There is no mutuality, no reciprocity, and no proper and meaningful care. Only one is living freely and there is no togetherness.

Relationships change, sometimes for the better, sometimes for the worse. Perhaps we can see this change most frequently as a drift, and this need not be a cause for concern. In togetherness there is no timetable, no rigid plan to adhere to; there is no route map. We offer each other space and so we have the freedom to change within the confines of togetherness and this means that the consequences of any change can remain limited and ameliorated by togetherness itself. But sometimes we might drift too far.

We remain two distinct people even as we see ourselves as one. We are distinct from the other even as we rely on them and never wish to leave them. We retain our independence and see the relationship as a mutual one. But this is because our commitment is seldom tested. It is not often we are in a situation where any serious sacrifice becomes necessary. Our sacrifices are often little ones: offering first use, doing things for, holding tight, listening, stopping what we are doing for a moment, always being there. These sacrifices are not reflected upon and might remain unacknowledged (until they stop happening), but they form the real basis of any relationship. The unconditionality of our duty to the other manifests itself in the ordinary reiteration of our actions. There is no great show. We only continue to demonstrate our duty in many little ways. We cannot afford for them to be deliberative. We have to take the unconditionality for granted so we can live freely.

Perhaps the most interesting writer on relationships is Emmanuel Swedenborg, who in works such as *Heaven and Hell*[9] and *Conjugial Love*,[10] considers the freedom that can be found in togetherness, but also the hugely detrimental and disabling effect of one party in a relationship seeking to control the other. Swedenborg is certainly a thinker of his time, wedded to the Enlightenment conception of rationality, but also the intellectual limitations with regard to gender and genetics.[11] Yet he provides an understanding of togetherness that is based on mutuality and not subjugation that was well before its time. So we can strip out the 18th century assumptions and look at what he has to say with an open mind.

For Swedenborg, togetherness, in the form of conjugial or marriage love, involves a conjoining on both body and mind, of the affective and the rational. Marriage, for Swedenborg, is the coming together of the two elements of the Divine, namely love (or affection) and wisdom (or rationality). These are the two essential elements, and like heat and light in the natural world, they come from a single source. Love and wisdom are the two ways in which the Divine is manifested in the world. Like heat and light, which come from the sun, these two elements of love and wisdom complement each other and this is precisely how a couple comes together in a harmonious relationship. Wisdom cannot operate without love and nor can love subsist without wisdom.

For Swedenborg, the essence of a relationship is mutuality. Each party completes the other by their sharing of themselves unconditionally. As he states in *Heaven and Hell*, 'marriage love and its pleasure consist of the intent of one belonging to the other, and of this being mutual and reciprocal'.[12] We belong to each other, but we are not owned. What we do is share ourselves with the other and this is because, 'sharing and the union that follows from it is the very inward pleasure that is called blessedness in marriage'.[13] He goes on: 'When one partner wants or loves what the other does, then there is a freedom for both, because all freedom stems from love'.[14] Swedenborg suggests that it is through mutuality that we become truly able to express our individuality.

But Swedenborg then goes on to consider the opposite of this mutuality, where one partner seeks to control the other:

> *Any love of control of one over the other utterly*
> *destroys marriage love and its heavenly pleasure ....*
> *A love of being in control in a marriage destroys this*

because the dominant partner simply wants his or
her will to be in the other, and does not want to
accept any element of the will of the other in return.
So it is not mutual, which means that there is no
sharing of any love and its pleasure with the other,
and no accepting in return.[15]

In order to control the other we have to subjugate them and this destroys their autonomy: 'Control subjugates, and a subjugated mind either has no purpose or is of opposite purpose. If it has no purpose it has no love, and if it is of opposite purpose there is hatred in place of love'.[16]

One need not accept Swedenborg's cosmology and theology to see the underlying point here, and we can use this as a framework for understanding how we can live together in some form of harmony. Conjugial love is where we are both free of ego. It is not about 'me' and it is not a concern for self-fulfilment or aspiration. It rather supposes a sublimation of the self into a greater whole. It depends on an acceptance of the other as they are and of complementing them. It is how we complete ourselves by joining with another. But what it cannot be is a controlling relationship: we cannot seek to use the other to further our own purposes and nor is it a competitive relationship where we put our ego with another.

The cause of control is ego. Vladimir Solovyov states that egoism should be distinguished from individuality. We are, Solovyov suggests, possessors of 'absolute significance and worth'.[17] He goes on to state that: 'In every human being there is something absolutely irreplaceable, and one cannot value oneself too highly ... Failure to recognise one's own absolute significance is equivalent to a denial of basic human worth'.[18] We are then to see ourselves as distinct individuals who have an intrinsic worth. But if we stop here we are left only with egoism, which is something Solovyov feels we should try to avoid:

> *The basic falsehood and evil of egoism lie not in this*
> *absolute self-consciousness and self-evaluation of the*
> *subject, but in the fact that, ascribing to himself in*
> *all justice an absolute significance, he unjustly*
> *refuses to others this same significance. Recognising*
> *himself as a centre of life (which as a matter of fact*
> *he is), he relegates others to the circumference of his*
> *own being and leaves them only an external and rel-*
> *ative value.*[19]

The error is not then to denigrate oneself, but to focus only on oneself and not to see others as being as significant as we are. In order words, egoism is where we only promote ourselves as worthwhile and ignore the other. The emphasis on our own worth relegates others to a subsidiary position whereby they are only seen from our orbit, from that position that most matters to us.

Togetherness, we might suggest, is an unconditional, one-sided commitment that works by being mutual. But the responsibility on each party is complete and total: we have an unending duty to the other. The commitment we have to each other is only reciprocated *because* it is total and unconditional. It has not ulterior motive and does not depend on the certainty of anything in return.

There is a particular chemistry in a relationship that develops out of its specific ingredients, and if it works then we can accept it and feel comfortable. We feel that it suffices and so have no need to look for an objective rule to measure it by, and this applies whether we are attracted to traditional or radical approaches to togetherness. We do not see the other as being an ideal type or as representative of a gender or type. Indeed, it may be a problem if we were to see them as such: they become a mere cipher for something else or perhaps even become seen as a trophy. Instead of an ideal, the reality of a relationship is that two distinct individuals with their own interests, experiences, attitudes and beliefs chose to come together to form a relationship that involves standing back at times, giving up things and doing things differently, all in order to create something that is greater than each of them. There is a specific mutuality that develops over time rather than accommodating to a pre-existing template. It involves putting the other first in the recognition that this enhances us as much as it does them.

So the key issue here is whether one person seeks to control the other. Does the ego of one dominate the other? The control, where it occurs, is always particular, and it derives out of the specifics of the lived experiences of two individuals. So while we may be able to point to the general problem of control, it will always manifest itself differently dependent on the nature of the relationship. We live by accommodating each other, and not according to abstract principles. If we tried to live by an abstract principle we would merely be controlling. It would mean the imposition of one particular view on to the other for an external purpose. If both parties share the principles and live by it naturally then there is no issue. Indeed one may have been attracted to another precisely because of a certain shared principle. It is entirely different for one party to impose their principles on another.

There are differing levels of control, some milder than others. It can be a form of slavery, but it might take rather gentler forms. We can explore this rather gentler form of control by focusing on what might appear to be a rather banal example. It is perhaps not uncommon for one person to say another that: 'I cannot live without you.' But what does it mean to say that we cannot live without somebody else?

Does it really mean that we will die if they were to go? Most often this is not really what is meant. What is meant is that our lives would be very different, perhaps unrecognisably so, were they not there. It is a situation we never wish to face, where there would be a great loss and we do not know if we could cope. We clearly think we might not. For the other to go would be a personally transformative situation. We might feel that there is now a gaping hole left in our lives that we feel can never again be filled. The person is irreplaceable and we would have to live in a profoundly different manner, which we might see as not worth living. We will have to question all we have taken for granted and become used to. We simply do not wish to live without that person.

But in reality, of course, we would go on living and we could still make much of our lives and remain doing much of what we did before. We may get over the loss of that person (and this undoubtedly may take time) or we may find someone else. Crucially our statement — 'I cannot live without you' — is hypothetical. We cannot really know how we will feel and what we would do. The statement is based on our current feelings, not on any possible future ones. It is a statement of what we have, not what we might not have. If it were to arise we might face the loss rather differently. Being left by someone might alter our perception of them: if someone we loved can really treat us in such a way then perhaps we were wrong about them.

The phrase, of course, is often intended merely as a statement of our fidelity. The phrase is a simple signal of our affection. It is to state that this person is simply the most important person to them and that they do not want to live without them. It is here a simple, if a rather dramatic statement of love, and meant to be taken as such. It is when it drifts into something more serious that we might see it as sinister. It then becomes an attempt to control and manage a

relationship and a person. It is where an ego seeks to dominate another and so there is no real togetherness.

When we claim that we cannot live without someone, no
matter how honestly we might mean it, we do not really
expect it to be tested. It is not meant as a challenge to the
other and we do not wish them to test us. But perhaps there
may be a time when it is said out of fear that the other may
actually leave. The phrase now becomes a form of emotional
blackmail. What we mean now is 'I will kill myself if you
leave me'. This is an entirely different matter. It is indeed a
threat, with a view to forcing someone to act in a particular
manner. How should we respond to this form of blackmail?
Can it ever be acceptable? Is it our problem, in the sense that
we should change our plans in the face of this threat? And
how can we — the person it is said to — judge, before the
fact, whether it is seriously meant? It remains still a hypothetical statement.

But what if we felt the phrase was being used to blackmail
us? Is this really the sort of person we would wish to be
with? Is someone who threatens to take their own life if we
do something against their will really worth being with?

Controlling another is to show a lack of care for that person. The other is being used and so the relationship no longer
works as if should for them. They are now in a relationship
with another not for their sake, but for the benefit of that
other person. They are not being looked after and there is no
mutuality. Another is using that person, forcing them to sacrifice themselves not to create something greater, but for the
benefit of that other person. Accordingly, the relationship
diminishes them. The relationship now serves the ego and is
based on selfishness.

Controlling, of course, need not be violent to be effective,
and nor need it be at such intense a level that the relationship
becomes impossible. It might be that the person controlling

the other is not being consciously cruel. They may not be aware of their actions, but see them as entirely normal, and indeed the other may come to do so as well. It may be that the apparent benefits of the relationship, say, in terms of physical and financial security, seem to outweigh the effects of the control. Or it might be that habit obscures the extent or even existence of the control: they have simply got used to acting in a particular manner and are not even aware that their life could now be otherwise.

Of course, it might be that the control actually takes the form of habits, and it can use the physical and financial security offered by the relationship. In this sense the control aspects of the relationship might be hard to disentangle from the affection that each party still shows to the other.

But even where the control remains non-violent, unconscious and even apparently harmless it is still a problem, because being together means the voluntary accommodation of another to create a greater whole. We believe that being together enhances each individual and develops them personally. Togetherness completes them in a very real sense. So for one to control another is to disable the other, to leave the relationship as partial and incomplete. Control is based on the delusion that a relationship can exist and stand on only one leg, with one part atrophied or withered.

VIII

The only way I continue to move is further into my interior. The more I think about dwelling and how we use it the deeper I go. I turn inwards reflecting on what most of us do without any reflection, and concerning myself with what causes most others very little concern. This may be taken as a fault. Some might suggest that I should get out more and that I might live a little more rather than thinking about the possibility of what happens when we are out and about. But I think not. As Franz Kafka said:

> *It isn't necessary that you leave home. Sit at your*
> *desk and listen. Don't even listen, just wait. Don't*
> *wait, be still and alone. The whole world will offer*
> *itself to you to be unmasked, it can do no other, it*
> *will writhe before you in ecstasy.*[20]

The world eventually gives itself up to us and all we have to do is wait. Simply living is world disclosing if only we are prepared to wait and look. So instead of being up and about, running to catch up with everyone else who is out there, I stay where I am and wait for the world to come to me.

But aren't academics meant to be outward looking beings? If you read people like William Mitchell or Paul Shepheard (whose work I enjoy) we can follow them from Melbourne to Paris, or Austin to Rome, stopping off at Harvard or Brisbane to teach some brilliant and challenging postgraduate students. Mitchell[21] makes much of the mobile wireless technology he takes with him and the mobility of the mind-set that allows him to see how the urban environment is changing. Shepheard traverses the globe teaching and instructing, even as he based the narrative of one of his books[22] on his extended family coming together for thanksgiving; a story, as it were, of a family finding its place in the world.

But this is not for me: travel may broaden the mind but I have always been one for depth. I was once challenged by a friend, as we fed him and his wife and the wine had flowed for a time, whether I really could know that much about dwelling when I had spent so long living in the same place. I bristled at this, especially as I had lived in 10 different dwellings before I was 14 years of age. But the best response I thought was to say simply that I had lived in dwellings all my life, and that nearly every day I had come home and so experienced what home is as distinct from what it is not. Perhaps the number of different dwellings we have lived in might matter to some, but for me the issues of permanence and security are rather more important.

To my mind, an academic of dwelling ought to stay at home, rather like Martin Heidegger using his mountain hut as the only place where he would write and make sense of the world.[23] I do not wish to grant my little 1980s suburban house anything like the romantic or even metaphysical grace that Heidegger gives his mountain hut, but it is still the place I need and seek to sequester myself in. It is where my books are, my notebooks, my laptop, my DVDs, CDs, all my inspirations and all the tools of my trade. But even more importantly, it is where my family are, and where all my traces, the routes and ruts of my ordinary life, can be found. The jet-setting life would destroy this; it would neuter what I have to say, and prevent my normal, established and desired form of expression.

Of course, this stasis on my part was not planned. I did not set out to live this way or to write in this manner. But this is precisely the boon of private dwelling: it accommodates us, and all it needs is for us to accept it. So once I found my place I wished to keep it, to stay there. I had no aspirations for it to be anything else, or to be anywhere else. I aimed, and have so far succeeded, to be always and forever in this one and only place. And it is the one and only place because of whom and what it contains. It is not merely me here, but those who would call me *mine*.

One of the main assets of private dwelling is that it leaves us with nothing to prove. Its utility is self-evident in our lack of any need for reflection on its evident utility. What convinces me that I know my dwelling is that I do not any longer have to notice it, such that when I do really look at it, as in stopping and focusing on an aspect of it, it takes me by surprise. It is a distinct and hard material object and it carries the distinctions of use and occasional misuse. It is a serious object in its construction and complexity. It shows signs of wear and it is different, in its way, from any other. This is because of those who can call it *mine*. It is the ties I have with this place that both helps to complete me and which also frees me. It is by the mutuality of the care that I share that I grow into a free being, knowing there is some protection and that I have some reason to grow. This care, which comes from living together, is only possible in a private and enclosed place. I don't have to reflect on it as a thing.

In any case, the ideal of a place relates only in a minor way to its amenity. What matters much more is the complacency found in its implacability, such that its indifference is both mine and benign. What makes for the ideal of place is the lack of reflection it needs to bear. There is no sense of contingency or conditionality. The measure of the ideal is the persistence of the place. The place never has cause to say 'but'.

This ideal, for me at least, came to depend on the infrequency of the starts and the duration of the stops. This was a function of the 10 different dwellings in my first fourteen years. Life for me was a continual round of new starts and short stops, as we moved from one place to another. To be in control of the starts and stops is all I ever wished for. Once I could insist that I stopped rather than being told to start over again I knew I could be free.

Of course, I appreciate that this has affected others. I really do not know if my children have benefitted or suffered from my need for stasis and complacency. Yes, they do still talk to me. But will they be able to build their own nest? Do they resent the lack of change and the constraints placed on them by sameness rather than change? After all, why should they see things as I do? They have not had the same formative experiences as me and cannot know how I felt as a child. Perhaps they will now relish change and contingency because it has been limited by my actions. They might now take every opportunity to move. What I hope I have given them is a place from which they can choose, and be free. And, for good measure, I have not put them through the dislocations that I had to suffer. I cannot regret this, whatever they may have inadvertently missed as a result.

As a child grows the relationship with their parents alters and the proximity they demand from a parent changes. It becomes less demonstrative, more passive, and there needs to be a certain physical distance. The change here can be difficult to judge, and is easy to misjudge. This physical distance is not a function of growing apart, or it need not be, but is rather a different sense of being together that relies on a shared store, and a tacit understanding of that store, rather than physical contact. We reserve the physical for other purposes — for the emergency, to reassure or console, or to reunite. The casualness of the parent-child relationship has gone and our children become our friends and confidantes if we are fortunate, while they seek closeness with another. The depth of love is undiminished, but must now manifest itself in a different and less demonstrative manner. We often have to trust that our children know that it is still there.

My children, now young adults, have more than one place they call home. They go from home to home, but even now when they are with us for only a few weeks at a time they retain the same easy manner of use, the same complacency and sense of belonging, that they had 10 years before. I would indeed be sad and worried if they did not still see it as theirs, as still part of what is ours. I want them to continue to see this place as theirs and it matters that they remain part of this place.

As they grow older we can share our past with our children and this, as I have found, fascinated them. There is a joy for both of us in talking about their grandmother (my mother) who they barely remember, and telling them things about myself and our family that they did not know, but are now old enough to appreciate. I am now able to bring them into that part of my life that preceded them. And now, when they are getting older and have left home, we have gaps in our knowledge of them. When they were children we knew all about them as they did everything with us. But now they are living independently and so we rely on them to tell us what they have done, who they have met and how they are feeling. Soon enough they will be able to tell stories to their children about people and things the latest generation know little of, but who I know so well.

IX

I began this chapter with a brief justification in which I suggested that there were a number of things I was reasonably certain of. First, I suggested that we live for long periods with the same people. As children we live with our parents until we become adults. We then, we hope, settle down with someone who, again we hope, will be our life's partner. This may result in having children ourselves who will stay with us until their adulthood. Not everyone will follow this route, but many will.

Second I stated that we live for long periods in the same place. Again, it may be that some of us, as I did in my childhood, are forced to move from place to place. This can occur for a number of reasons and not all of them need be anything like traumatic or even problematical. Yet, for many of us, we will stay in the same place for an extended period of time, which may last several decades. We make this place as we want it to be and will share it with those people we connect to. This raises the third point: both these people and these places matter to us very much. We come to know these people so well because we can exclude others and enclose them with ourselves in our special place. This place, in turn, becomes special in large part because of who we share it with. It becomes a special place because it is shared and because this sharing endures. We can do this because of the fourth point: most of us live like this at the same time, but we do so apart. Indeed, we use these people and places to separate ourselves from other people and places that we have no connection with. And we all do this.

The fifth point is that in order to understand why these people and places matter to us we have to experience them as they actually are. This means we have to see them, so to speak, when they are not being observed by those with no connection to the people or the place. We cannot observe this situation in an objective manner and expect it to be real. An outside observer would prevent us acting as we would choose to if we could exclude them, and there is no way of getting around this fact. Accordingly, our last statement is that we have no alternative but to rely on lived experience and anecdote. We can only use certain subjective approaches that come out of our own experiences inside dwelling and through sharing that exclusive space.

This chapter has derived out of two particular places. First, there is the place that I share with those people I love. My relationships with these people in this place are the primary material for this chapter. These relationships could only be formed and sustained by excluding everyone else, and this dramatically reduces the number of people who can corroborate my argument. The second place is on that is even more exclusive: my own headspace. This chapter has come out of how I have interpreted my memories, my experiences, my reading and my connections. It cannot be corroborated. There is no means of getting at this place without the mediation of my own will and understanding, or in other words what I am prepared to say and write down. Even those I share the other place with cannot get into this space. If they wish to know what is in there they have to trust what I say I am thinking, feeling and writing, and in this sense they are in the same position as any other reader of this chapter. Of course, they have shared many of the experiences, but they cannot prevent me from interpreting them as I will and making something significant from them.

But this situation only mirrors the subject matter of this chapter. We can know something of those we share with, and we know more than those outside can ever do. But this remains limited by how we interact and what we choose to share and hold back. It is this very sense of the subjective that I have hoped to capture here. But this means that the reader has to trust the author in a manner that may not be that comfortable for many readers, particularly those trained in the social scientists. But I am afraid that I can offer no real comfort here. It seems to me that there is simply no proper alternative to this approach. There is no way that an outsider can see what I can see, just as I cannot see what I am excluded from. We can rely on fictional accounts, but these are always prepared with some motive in mind: the author or director is always attempting to say something that is *public*. But what we wish to know about are precisely those things that are without motive and which, by definition, cannot be made public and continue to exist. We therefore have to rely on what others tell us and hope that we ourselves can be believed.

The grim conclusion to this is perhaps 'take it or leave it'. If one is prepared to accept these limitations then that is welcome. But if not, then I am afraid that there is nothing else to be said.

NOTES

1. King (2004).

2. King (2017).

3. King (2008).

4. King (2017).

5. King (2004, 2008).

6. Solovyov (1985).

7. *Ibid.*, p. 42.

8. Shepheard (1997).

9. Swedenborg (2010).

10. Swedenborg (1996).

11. Swedenborg lived from 1688 until 1772.

12. Swedenborg (2010), p. 217 (S. 380.1).

13. Op. cit.

14. Swedenborg (2010) p. 217 (S.380.2).

15. *Ibid.*, p. 217 (S. 380. 1).

16. *Ibid.*, p. 217 (S. 380.2).

17. Solovyov (1985), p. 42.

18. *Ibid.*, pp. 42–43.

19. *Ibid.*, p. 43.

20. Kafka (2006), p. 108.

21. Mitchell (2003).

22. *Artificial Love* (2003).

23. Sharr (2006).

ALONE AND TOGETHER

The sea is pacifying: it calms us and we can just sit and watch and listen to it. H, having spent the morning splashing around on the beach, is now more conscious of her place in the world and wishes to be more dignified, and so she has found a good place to sit on a rock surrounded on three sides by the sea.

As H sat there she could look out to sea and see nothing else. She could avoid all land, ignore all other people and just reflect passively on the regularity of the waves and take her thoughts just as they came, gentle wave after gentle wave. More than once I had done the same, just sitting and looking out to sea. Like her, I had listened to the waves rolling the pebbles backwards and forwards across the beach, or, on other occasions, watched the sea beating hard and angrily against a harbour wall, crashing in and, with a reluctant whoosh, falling back down, only to come back and try again.

In a place like this time seems to operate in a different manner, based no longer on the regularity of the clock, on artificial man-made time, but instead we begin to move according to the rhythm of the waves with their ebb and flow, the regular forward and back. The flow is, of course, in one sense irregular, as the tide is always going in or going out, encroaching or receding, each wave a tiny increment on what went before. It seems to build up — 'Every seventh wave is a big one', I remember telling H and her sister when they were tiny standing up to their ankles in the sea — and then, for a time, to recede.

Waves help us with our thoughts. Their regularity can help us internalise things, to get lost in ourselves. There is a quality to thought that comes from having apparently limitless time, that there is nothing else in the way to prevent us from just sitting there in that place with those thoughts. This offers a delicious feeling of possibility. Yet it also depends on place, on having the solitude and capability of being alone. What seems to matter is the openness of time, and this comes from place.

So I know how H felt as she sat on that rock looking out to sea, wanting to be left alone, even as she knew her family were near and would stay near. I have described this sense of being alone with others around as *companionable solitude*.[1] It is where we are within the reach of others, and feel them around us, but they do not actively engage with us. We know they are there, and we know they can see us and help us if we call. And this helps us to be alone. We were there on the next rock, in calling range, but keeping our distance, giving H the space to think and to breathe her own air. In this calmness, this pacific air, she can be herself, think her own thoughts and try to work things out.

H sat there for over half an hour, without anyone coming near. Once a stranger with his camera ready to take a shot of the sea innocently came too close, but backed off when he saw the look of trespass on H's face. We knew better and so clambered on to nearby rocks and spent some time ourselves staring out to sea.

We signalled to H that we wanted to leave. For a while she pretended to ignore us, before she finally stood up. But instead of joining us she decided she wanted to get even closer to the sea. This would involve her edging down a near vertical 10-foot drop with only the smallest of footholds. We called to her to stop, getting ever more insistent and unable to keep an edge of parental anxiety out of our voices, until she finally turned and said 'OK, if it makes you feel better'. She climbed back up off the rocks, moving past us and, ignoring our attempts to give her a significant look, she headed off towards the beach. She had found her place and would now leave it as she wished.

When things are as they should be, when they seem to be all right, we say that things are all *in place*. Things are where they should be; they are ready, well ordered, as we would want them to be. We would say it about an army preparing for battle, a team on the field before the start of play, actors ready to come on stage, or of someone comfortable with where and what they are.

This little phrase — *in place* — carries with it a sense of preparedness. It implies a properness, a propriety, a manner, position or condition that is necessary or correct, and when this is achieved there is an order. Hence the phrase 'remember your place', where we seek to remind someone of their rank, of their place in a hierarchy, of their relative position compared to us. This relativity is important: it is not an absolute position but one dependent on a particular structure, system or set of ways and the places of others within it. The use of the phrase is normally to suggest that someone is seeking a place higher than they really deserve or higher than others think should pertain: it can be taken to mean that we should get out of where we currently are and go back to another place where we more properly belong. We are being accused of over-reaching.

There is a sense here that we always have a level, that there is somewhere that is more properly ours. There is a level that is correct for us. This may be a recognition of the limits of our talents or our competence or it might be the place where we are most comfortable, playing in one position rather than another, taking one role in a firm and not another. To say to another that they should know their place can be meant, and taken, as an insult or as a criticism for when we are seen as over-reaching or encroaching.

But it can just as well refer to an understanding of our nature and our capabilities. It is where we know *our* place. Yes, this might be because of what we have been told. Yet it might be due to self-realisation and experience, to an understanding that in some place we can be just as we wish or are meant to be. Sometimes we find the rock that is just right for us.

There is also a more general sense in which we have for being in place. If we are to be what we want to be, if we are to be at all, then we have to be located. If we are to be with others then they too should be located. To be is to understand that they and us need and should have *our* place which is also always *mine* for each one of us. It is this understanding that gives an order to our being. It allows us to seek comfort in ourselves and in others, where the spaces are known. We can maintain our bearings; we can retain some level of stability and stasis, and through this we can develop an understanding of our surroundings and ourselves. We can do this because our idea of place is of something that is bounded. Our sense of place is contained and limited and so it provides us with the means of separation, even if we are still with others and want them to be there. So to say a place is ours is for it to become bounded space, a space of differentiation.

This becomes all too clear when we consider the opposite of 'in place', where we are *out of place*. Clearly we are still in some place in that we remain located in space. Yet the place is not where we are meant to be. We are not in our 'proper' place, where we are at peace, or where we belong or feel comfortable. We are out of that place that we feel is ours. We are there only on sufferance, or by mischance and fear that once we are found out we will be removed or that perhaps even something worse will become of us.

Clearly this place may actually be where we want to be. It might be somewhere or with someone we deeply desire; it may be our life's ambition. Yet it is a place where we just do not fit. We appear as an outsider, as someone who should not be there. Of course, the decision might not be ours. We might wish to be here, and indeed see ourselves as being here, but it is not for us to say. There are others who guard the boundary and it is off limits to us. We feel out of place because of how others react or relate to us, so that while we can feel we should be there in that place, others may not accept this and ignore or abuse us. They reject us and leave us alone in a crowded or occupied place. We are out of *our* place and in the place of another. We are the proverbial fish out of water, out of our natural environment. We have an environment, we have a place where we can and perhaps should go, but we just do not know it or wish to accept it.

This is important, in that it reminds us that being in place is not just a question of where we are, but also where we are not. It is a matter of where we can be and where we cannot be. It also alerts us to the fact that we are never not is some place or other. Being out of place is where we are not accepted or permitted to be where we currently are. This may mean we have to go home to our proper place. However, there may be no place where we are accepted, where we can be properly in place. We may have no place that is properly *mine*, even as we remain in this place that is not ours. But in this condition we are not located, not secure because we are not entitled to be there.

Like H, we can stay in a certain place because no one stops us. If another person were sitting on her rock then she would have had to share it — if she dared — or go elsewhere. So it was a chance finding, a place ready for her when she wanted it. But also the place, or rather its utility, depended entirely on H's readiness to use it. It had no intrinsic quality: its quality derived from H's readiness to use it there and then.

H did not search for the right rock; it was just there ready. At that time, in that place, when she needed to be alone to ponder it was just there. We might even say that the rock, in its implacable way, found her. This fits better: H did nothing but turn up. She created nothing and controlled nothing, not the rock, not the tide. It was just there ready for her use, a serendipitous rock, pure time and place.

A rock, like the sea, is elemental. It could not be made by H, by the particular individual in that time and that place. But that particular person created the place as individual to her. She did this by her presence, by her dwelling. It was her particularity that gave rise to it as place, and which has offered it a meaning. Dwelling, we might say, manifests the place.

It is our place to be alone and to be together: to be within and to be without. We know, as H did, that we can be alone while we are still with others; and we also know we can be together when those who love and care for us are physically far away. Knowing this allows us to remain in place, and to use that place, to come together or to move apart, to preserve our relations or to maintain our separation. And so we go on.

NOTE

1. King (2008).

BIBLIOGRAPHY

Bachelard, G. (1969). *The poetics of space*. Boston, MA: Beacon.

Beck, U. (1992). *The risk society: Towards a new modernity*. London: Sage.

Elster, J. (Ed.). (1986). *Rational choice*. Oxford: Blackwell.

Elster, J. (1999). *Strong feelings: Emotion, addiction and human behaviour*. Cambridge, MA: MIT Press.

Freud, S. (2008). *The interpretation of dreams*. Oxford: Oxford University Press.

Heidegger, M. (1962). *Being and time*. Oxford: Blackwell.

Kafka, F. (2006). *Zurau aphorisms*. London: Harvill Secker.

Kierkegaard, S. (2004). *The sickness unto death: A Christian psychological exposition for edification and awakening* (p. 141). London: Penguin.

King, P. (1996). *The limits of housing policy: A philosophical investigation*. London: Middlesex University Press.

King, P. (2004). *Private dwelling: Contemplating the use of housing*. London: Routledge.

King, P. (2008). *In dwelling: Implacability, exclusion and acceptance*. Aldershot: Ashgate.

King, P. (2017). *Thinking on housing: Words, memories, use.* Abingdon: Routledge.

Lachman, G. (2013). *The* caretakers of the cosmos: Living responsibly in an unfinished world. Edinburgh: Floris Books.

Mitchell, W. (2003). *Me + +: The cyborg self and the networked city.* Cambridge, MA: MIT Press.

Porter, R., & Dunant, S. (Eds.) (1997). *Age of anxiety.* London: Virago.

Salecl, R. (2004). *On anxiety.* London: Routledge.

Sharr, A. (2006). *Heidegger's hut.* Cambridge, MA: MIT Press.

Shepheard, P. (1997). *The cultivated wilderness: Or what is landscape?* Cambridge, MA: MIT Press.

Shepheard, P. (2003). *Artificial love: A story of machines and architecture.* Cambridge, MA: MIT Press.

Solovyov, V. (1985). *The meaning of love.* New York, NY: Lindisfarne Press.

Swedenborg, E. (1987). *Divine love and wisdom.* London: Swedenborg Society.

Swedenborg, E. (1996). *Conjugial love.* London: Swedenborg Society.

Swedenborg, E. (2010). *Heaven and hell.* West Chester: Swedenborg Foundation.

INDEX